# Daniel

## His Godly Lifestyle

# DANIEL

*His Godly Lifestyle*

## Dennis L Clark

## www.dennisclarkministries.com

Paint Basket Ltd

# Copyright Notice

## Main Text
### Taken from the Authorized King James Version


### All quotes are from the
# HOLY BIBLE
# NEW INTERNATIONAL
# VERSION ®
### Copyright © 1073, 1978, 1984 by the International Bible Society.
### Used by permission.


### Front Cover Design:   D.L. Clark

### Cover Photograph:
ID 3020350 © Mikhail Levit |
Dreamstime.com


### Published by the Author
### 247 Glamorgan Drive, Torbay,
### North Shore City
### Auckland, New Zealand.

# Contents

# Preface

## *The CB Radio (Citizen Band)*

During the 1970's the mobile transmitter hit South Africa with a mighty bang! Soon nearly every house had a ¼ wave antenna on its roof. Illegal antennae, such as the Yagi, 5/8 wave, and others, were cunningly hidden in back gardens, away from the prying eyes of Post Office Officials. Every second car sported a CB antenna. Those "in the know" were regularly warned of speed traps, of the wires "tying the pavements together".

It was the days of Good Buddies and 10-4's.
The airways buzzed with excitement as literally thousands of budding "Amateur Radio Hams" verbally fought each other for space on the highly overcrowded and ridiculously few channels allocated by Post Office Regulations. These channels were fully occupied 24 hours a day.

In order to bring some type of order to the chaotic situation, "Channel Masters" tried to organize groups in such a way that, where possible, each CB'er would have a chance to be spoken to, and also to speak to others on the channel without interference. In general the airways were absolutely chaotic.

It was in this environment that early one morning a deep booming voice erupted over the airways with a loud "Praise the Lord!" That was Harold Barker, alias, "HAROLD THE BISHOP". He soon was soon asked to open the channel "meeting" with a short Scripture reading.

On another channel I was invited to do the same. One morning someone asked me why I did not give a short comment on the verses being read.
That was the start of the:

## *CB CHRISTIAN CORNER*

This eventual became known over several parts of the world. The messages soon lengthened from a few minutes to a standard of between 20 to 25 minutes in length.

Many knew me only by my CB name or "handle" of UNCLE RUFUS (Romans 16:13 ....*Rufus, chosen of the Lord...*). Shortly after this John Horn alias JOHN 3 - ( from John3:16; *For God so loved the world that* .....) of Germiston became my very able helper

12

and between the two of us, with occasional help from others, we brought the Gospel Message of Jesus Christ every day of the week for just over ten years.

Many were led to the Lord Jesus Christ, many were counselled, many were prayed for, and many were the times when we were called out in the middle of the night to help those who were in distress.

We very often had to visit the various hospitals to pray for the sick and the dying. We ministered Holy Communion to people in their homes, some were at the point of death, while their own shepherds had not heeded their cry from the soul. For many disabled people, and pensioners, the CB Christian Corner was their only "church".

This book is a direct result of those days on the CB and was originally brought over the air as a series of short messages. It has always been my desire to bring those messages over into book form.

Two previous series have already been published off-line and are registered in the Republic of South Africa State Library. These books are as follows:

**Studies in the Book of ZECHARIAH** – The Prophet of Hope and Mercy - first Edition 1995. ISBN 0-620-20461-3

**The Seven Great I Am's** (booklet) - first Edition 1996 – ISBN 0-620-20460-5

Sometime in the future I hope to publish these as eBooks as well.

My special thanks to my wife Anna for the times she was alone while I spent long hours at the computer and word processor and researching material. May the Lord continue to bless her in abundance.

I also wish to thank the following persons who so kindly offered to spend time proof-reading and reviewing this publication. To them, many thanks for their constructive criticism advice and help.

**Pastor Joe Hawley** of the Word and Life AFM Church (Apostolic Faith Mission) Church in Boksburg.

Dr Pieter Oldewage. Pastor of the Balfour AFM Church in Mpumalanga, and

John Clark, my brother, of Memel, Orange Free State.

Sannie du Toit, Crossroads Christian Congregation, Browns Bay, New Zealand

Dennis L. Clark
2015

# INTRODUCTION

**Daniel 1:1-4**

*1. In the third year of the reign of Jehoiakim king of Judah came Nebuchadnezzar king of Babylon unto Jerusalem and besieged it.*

*2. And the Lord gave Jehoiakim king of Judah into his hands, with part of the vessels of the house of God: which he carried into the land of Shinar to the house of his god: and he brought the vessels into the treasure house of his god.*

*3. And the king spake unto Ashpenaz the master of his eunuchs, that he should bring certain of the children of Israel, of the king's seed and the princes:*

*4. Children in whom there was not blemish, but well favoured, and skilled in all wisdom, and cunning in knowledge, and understanding science, and such as had the ability in them to stand in the king's palace. And whom they might teach the learning and the tongue of the Chaldeans.*

The Book of Daniel is a very interesting one, and we will not be looking at the prophetic side of his life [this is not the subject of this book], but rather at his life style and how he lived.

We will, however, study in detail one of his visions.

Firstly, we will look at his youth, how he acted as a young boy; and we will be concentrating on Daniel 1:4

Many people today tend to look down at youngsters who serve the Lord with all their heart and their soul and with all their might. It gives me great encouragement when I see the little ones praising Jesus. In one of my previous congregations I belonged to we had many 7 – 10 year old children serving and praising Jesus such that it would put many a grown-up to shame.

We older ones tend to be very conservative and say that emotion should not be part of our religious life, that we are to be prim and proper, that it is just not right to laugh or cry before the Lord. Just read the Scriptures to see just how the great men of God acted and reacted before the presence of God.

They acted with great emotion: sometimes dancing before the Lord, sometimes shouting and singing loudly, other times just being quiet. If the world can become excited at their worship of worldly things, so

much more should Christians become excited about the things of the Lord!
When that happens we will have revival in our land and God will bless abundantly.

Daniel stood for his faith and his God, so let us take a look just how he reacted to circumstances beyond his control.

# Chapter 1

## 1. Daniel in Exile

Daniel came from Judea, i.e., the area from just north of Jerusalem right down to just south of the city of Beersheba. The Babylonians had taken him and his friends as prisoners just before the main group of exiles. Daniel obviously came from the higher aristocracy and most probably was one of noble or royal descent. What was certain of these boys is that they were of exceptional intelligence and upbringing.

It is said that Daniel was approximately 16 years of age when he was taken captive and that he spent altogether 69 years in Babylon. One thing is certain, that in spite of the idolatry of the nation, and its terrible vileness, Daniel stayed clean and pure in the service of his Lord and God. I think this is a great lesson for us in these days.

We are so often put under great temptations to serve the world that we need to read up the lives of those men and women who have stayed close to the Lord in times of great tribulation. For example, just think and pray for the Christians right now in countries where they suffer and are persecuted, and sometimes die, for their faith in Jesus Christ.

# 2. Daniel and his Examination

Daniel and his companions were put through a selection committee, if you can call it that, because the king of Babylon had put certain qualifications to who may, or may not, serve before him. There were six qualifications that applied to Daniel and his companions, so let us take a look at them and see how they apply to us today!

## 2.1 They had to have no physical defects

As a priest in the service of God the believer has to have no spiritual defects. It is impossible for the human to be completely free from physical defects. There was only one Person who was, and that was Jesus. He had to have no blemishes at all to have been the prefect sacrifice for our sins. Because of the perfect sacrifice His blood covers us and imputes to us His righteousness. This can only be if we ask forgiveness for our sins and let Jesus in as Saviour of our lives.

## 2.2 They had to be handsome and good-looking

Now just how does the Christian become handsome and good-looking for men, and beautiful in the case of women, especially when we know that every day we see people who are not.

I have personally seen, and knew, a pilot in World War 2 who had severe third degree burns all over his body and face. He seldom came out in public because of his disfigurement. If you looked at him you would certainly not call him handsome and good-looking.

Just how then does the Christian become handsome and good-looking – and I am speaking of ALL believers in Christ?

Paul, writing to the believers in Corinth said this in 2 Cor 2:15-16, *"For we are to God the aroma of Christ among those who are being saved and those who are perishing. To one we are the smell of death; to the other; the fragrance of life."* (NIV)

When we offer ourselves to God we become a sweet smelling savour to Him. You see, God does not look at the external face of the believer. He looks at the heart, the intentions of the heart.

Are you a sweet smelling savour to Jesus?

## 2.3 They had to have an aptitude to ANY kind of learning

## 2.4 They had to be well informed

I am going to handle these two points as one unit because they are linked. The believer has to know what is going on in the world: otherwise he/she will not know what to fight against or how to fight it. Many say that we have to just concentrate on the Word of God and become a hermit to the world. God did not intend it that way. If you become a hermit how can you ever lead others to Christ and to a saving knowledge of Him? No! You are in the world but should not be of the world.

Know what Satan is doing around you; that is the only way that you can effectively pray and fight against the spiritual forces. Also, and most importantly, know the Scriptures. Study them carefully and hide them in your heart. Paul told Timothy, another young man, *"Do your best to present yourself to God as one approved, a workman who does not need to be ashamed and CORRECTLY* [emphasis mine] *handles the word of truth"*. (2 Tim 2:15) The KJV states, *"Study to shew thyself approved unto God."*

How is your learning? Are you correctly informed? Are you using the information and learning you have gained?

### 2.5   They had to be quick to understand

Here is an important point in the life of the Christian believer. Many read the Scriptures without understanding a word of what God is trying to tell them. The worldly person reads it with worldly understanding only, but the Christian has to read it another way.

The only way the Bible can be read, if a proper understanding is to be attained, is with the help of the Holy Spirit to guide you. He, the Holy Spirit, was the author and He is the only one to help us. Paul spoke on this subject to the Corinthians. In 1 Cor 2:10-14 we read, *"The Spirit searches all things, even the deep things of God. For who among men knows the thoughts of a man except the man's spirit within him?"*

In the same way, no-one knows the thoughts of God except the Spirit of God.

*"We have not received the spirit of the world but the Spirit who is from God, that we may understand what God has freely given us. This is what we speak, not the words taught us by human wisdom but in words taught by the Spirit, expressing spiritual truths in spiritual words. The man without the Spirit does not accept the things that come from the Spirit of God., for they are foolishness to him, and he cannot discern them, because they are spiritually discerned."* 1 Cor 2:12-14 (NIV)

Are you trying to discern God's truths through your own spirit, or are you being guided by the Spirit of Jesus?

Lastly:

### 2.6 They had to be qualified to serve

In Ezekiel chapter 44 we read on what a priest in the service of the Lord should be like and how he is to serve the Lord. Every believer is a priest in the service of the Lord. How effective and just how priestly your life is depends on just how close you are to the Lord Jesus Christ, and just how much you let the Holy Spirit work in your life.

**Comment:**
What we have here can be likened to a University Entrance Examination for Daniel and his companions and they came through with flying colours - why?

There was only one reason.

They were, from tiny children, taught in the ways of the Lord: they were  taught to serve Him with reverence and with respect; they were taught to live a holy life, not to just read about it and leave it at that.

Praise the Lord that they were faithful and obedient. Praise the Lord that they had parents who lead them in the right direction. How do we shape up in this respect?

Now let us read further in the Book of Daniel:

**Daniel 1:5-16**
>     5.    And the king appointed them a daily provision of the king's meat, and the wine which he drank: so nourishing them three

*years, that at the end thereof they might stand before the king.*

*6.     Now among these were the children of Judah, Daniel, Hananiah, Mishael, and Azariah:*

*7.     Unto whom the prince of the eunuchs gave names: for he gave unto Daniel the name of Belteshazar; and to Hananiah, of Shadrach; and to Mishael of Meshach; and to Azariah of Abednego.*

*8.     But Daniel purposed in his heart that he would not defile himself with the portion of the king's meat; nor with the wine which he drank: therefore he requested of the prince of the eunuchs that he might not defile himself.*

*9.     Now God had brought Daniel into favour and tender love with the prince of the eunuchs.*

*10.    And the prince of the eunuchs said unto Daniel, I fear my lord the king, who hath appointed your meat and your drink: for why should he see your faces worse liking than the children which are of your sort? Then shall ye make me endanger my head to the king.*

*11.    Then said Daniel to Melzar, whom the prince of the eunuchs had set over Daniel, Hananiah, Mishael and Azariah*

*12.    Prove thy servants, I beseech thee, ten days; and let them give us pulse to eat and water to drink.*

*13.    Then let our countenances be looked upon before thee, and the countenances of the children that eat of the portion of the king's*

*meat: and as thou seest, deal with thy*
*servants.*
*14. So he consented to them in this matter,*
*and proved them ten days.*
*15. And at the end of ten days their*
*countenance appeared fairer and fatter in*
*flesh than all the children which did eat the*
*portion of the king's meat.*
*16. Thus Melzar took away the portion of*
*their meat, and the wine that they should*
*drink; and gave them pulse.*

King Nebuchadnezzar knew exactly what he wanted and he was determined to get whatever he wanted. He needed new blood in his service so he gave an order to his chief of the court officials to select and train some of the royal and upper class slaves from his recent triumph over the country of Israel.

The training that Daniel and his companions had to undergo was certainly one that was fairly extensive. Many of our degree and diploma training courses cover a three year period and if any of you have been through one or more, you will know just how much work and how many assignments are involved. They were to also be examined after the three year period to see if they had produced the fruit of their training.

The examiner was none other than the king himself. To be able to do this it is obvious that the king himself was a very educated man, otherwise he would not be able to judge if they were suitably trained or not. It is also significant to note that the disciples of Jesus had a three year training before Jesus was satisfied that they were able to perform the work of leading others into God's kingdom when He would no longer be on earth.

I put out a challenge to you: If you are a Christian of more than three years standing, are you trained in the Word of God? Or are you still a spiritual babe as mentioned in 1 Cor 3:2 where Paul admonished: *"Brothers, I could not address you as spiritual but as worldly – mere infants in Christ. I gave you milk, not solid food, for you were not yet ready. You were still worldly. For since there is jealousy and quarrelling among you, are you not worldly?"* (NIV)

## *What's in a name?*

Daniel and his three companions, Hananiah, Mishael and Azariah were only part of a group for training.

The name Daniel means **"God is my Judge"**, an expression that means that each person having this name is one who walks a sanctified life and only God can be the judge of whether he has in fact lived a pure life or not.

Similarly, Hananiah means **"Jehovah is gracious"** or **"Gift of the Lord"**. We will see just how gracious God was to him. In his conduct he was truly a gift of the Lord.

Mishael means **"High place"**, which in turn means an altar. Is name also means **"One who is like God is"**. This is surely a compliment to his style of living; a life pleasing to God Himself.

Lastly: Azariah means **"Jehovah is keeper"** or **"Jehovah is my helper"**, both really meaning the same thing. If God keeps you He is also your helper.

All these young men were, by virtue of their names, dedicated to Jehovah by their parents, but now king Nebuchadnezzar gives them new names. Why did he do this? The answer is simple. The king wanted to assimilate or absorb them into his own culture, that of Babylon. Their Hebrew names would always be a reminder of their past. New Babylonian names would make them part of the culture.

Names given to people of the East had, and mostly have, a meaning which corresponds to their nature or way of living. If God had to give you a name, what would be yours? Would it be one that glorifies Jesus? Or would it be one that tells everyone that you are of the world, in your way of living? The name that God will give you will depend on your choice of living.

Before you came to Jesus you had a name that the world has given you. When you came to Jesus and He became your Saviour and King, He gave you a new name and that is the name that He writes in His Book, the Book of the Lamb! (Rev 2:17) Exactly what that name is we will find out one day.

These young men were of the kingdom of Judah: Judah meaning **"The object of praise"** or **"Praise the Lord"**. We will also see that indeed they would be the object of the Lord's praise.

We have looked at Daniel in exile, and Daniel's examination, and now, thirdly, we have Daniel's decision.

## 3. Daniel's Decision

What was the decision that Daniel had to take? Verse 8 says, *"But Daniel resolved not to defile himself with royal food and wine, and he asked the chief official for permission not to defile himself this way. "* (NIV) Daniel wanted to continue to live the clean and pure life that he was used to. When one is in company of other who do not defile themselves it is easy to conform.

When, however, the Christian continues for a while to keep himself wilfully in the company of people who drink in excess, who swear and blaspheme the name of the Lord, etc., then that Christian, even with the best of intentions not to, eventually starts to do the things that are displeasing to the Lord. If he does not withdraw in time he will eventually become a backslider and will find it very difficult to come back to the Lord. Depending on circumstances he may even lose his salvation.

One thing we ought to take encouragement from

Daniel, and we ought to copy him, is the fact that he was not afraid to take his stand for the Lord, even in the most difficult of circumstances. He had the courage to stand for his convictions.

Do you take an open stand for Jesus at your work? Or elsewhere? Do others know you as a Christian, not in name only, but in practice? Remember, a tree is known by its fruit!

## 4. Daniel's Suggestion

When Daniel heard that they were to be given royal wine and food (meat) from the king's table he did not just summarily refuse to eat it. He acted with great wisdom. If he had not done that, he would have drawn the king's wrath down upon himself and his other Hebrew companions. At such a young age God had given Daniel wisdom beyond his age group and Daniel used it when he came with a suggestion as an alternative to what was planned for them.

Do you come up with wise alternatives when you are put to test by the world? Do you come up with an alternative at all? Or do you just give in?

When the chief official was not inclined to his suggestion Daniel came up with another suggestion. One thing about Daniel, he was not giving in without a struggle, and he knew God was on his side. He asked to be tested for 10 days. If after that, the official was not satisfied, we are not told what Daniel had next in mind. What we do know is that

God favoured Daniel and his companions to such an extent that they were allowed to eat food that did not defile themselves in God's sight.

If we are tested at any stage at all, I wonder just how we all would fare? It is easy to say that we will not fail. Remember Peter had all the good intentions, yet he failed Jesus when he denied Him three times. We need to ask ourselves if we are consistent in our Christian walk.

We also need to ask ourselves whether we are walking in the fruit of the Spirit; if we are exercising all of it, namely; *love, joy, peace, patience, kindness, goodness, faithfulness, gentleness and self-control* (Galatians 5:22) All of them ought to be present in our life, not just some of them.

Daniel practised all of them and he and his fellow Hebrew friends were honoured by God for their faithfulness and their obedience. He gave them knowledge and understanding of all kinds of literature and learning. Daniel was just a human being as ourselves, and if we follow Jesus with all of our heart and with all of our soul and all of our strength, then God will also give us what He gave Daniel.

Let me take you to James 1:5-6, *"If any of you lack wisdom, he should ask God, who gives generously to all without finding fault, and it will be given him. But when he asks, he must believe and not doubt." (NIV)*

Daniel did not doubt at any stage and he believed implicitly in his God, the living God of Abraham, Isaac and Jacob. Jesus is the same yesterday, today, and tomorrow. He is the One to model our lives on. Do it today and you will be blessed in abundance!

**Daniel 1:16-21**

> 16.   Thus Melzar took away the portion of the king's meat: and the wine that they should drink; and gave them pulse.
>
> 17.   As for these four children, God gave them knowledge and skill in all learning and wisdom, and Daniel had understanding in all visions and dreams
>
> 18.   Now at the end of the days that the king had said he should bring them in, then the prince of the eunuchs brought them in before Nebuchadnezzar.
>
> 19.   And the king communed with them, and among them all was none found like Daniel, Hananiah, Mishael, and Azariah: therefore stood they before the king.
>
> 20.   And all the matters of wisdom and understanding, that the king inquired of them, he found them ten times better than all the magicians and astrologers that were in all his realm.
>
> 21.   And Daniel continued even unto the first year of king Cyrus.

Let us consider, among other things, the matter of eating meat. Just what was the fuss all about? God, in the Old Testament, had told His people not to eat meat that had not been drained of blood. Many nations and cultures still eat and drink the blood of animals in direct contradiction to God's command.

God told Noah in Genesis 9:4, *"But you must not eat meat that has its lifeblood still in it. And for your lifeblood I will demand an accounting from every animal. And from each man, too. I will demand an accounting for the life of his fellow man." (NIV)*

Of interest here is that God will also demand an account from the animals that take a life (of man?) This statement is worth investigating at a later date. Exactly what God means here I do not know, but it is something to meditate on.

Verse 16 is not an advocate to become a vegetarian. What God is saying he is that meat without blood in it can be eaten. Daniel knew that he was in a godless society and he did not want to eat meat that had been dedicated, or sacrificed, to foreign gods. Another thing to take account is the fact that the Hebrews were prohibited from certain types of animals that were called "unclean."

But what about the Christian in the New Testament setting? Paul, in 1 Corinthians chapter 8, gives sound advice about the meat situation. If you are in any doubt, then study it carefully.

Jesus also said in Mark 7:14, *"Listen to me, everyone, and understand this. Nothing OUTSIDE* [emphasis mine] *a man can make him "unclean" by going into him. Rather, it is what comes OUT* [emphasis mine] *of a man that makes him "unclean"* [emphasis mine]. Jesus later explained to His disciples, *"Don't you see that nothing that enters a man from the outside can make him "unclean"? for it doesn't go into his heart but into his stomach, and then goes out of his body. (In saying this, Jesus declares all food 'clean')." (NIV)*

Don't get hung up on the Halaal sign on some of the foods. Boycott them, if you must, but if you have no option but to eat some, then remember, *"The One who is in you is greater that he who is in the world!"*

## 5. Daniel's Reward

Let's go back to Daniel 1:17.

All four of these youngsters had been given the gift of knowledge and of understanding, but Daniel had been given another "special" gift, the gift of interpreting dreams. God gives us gifts for the occasion and here God knew that Daniel would be using that gift to show His wonders to the world. God gives us gifts for the occasion today too. As Daniel was rewarded, so God gives gifts to those who love Him and worship Him.

In their training we are not told how the four were not involved in the magical arts, astrology, and the other things forbidden by God, but we do know that they kept themselves pure and loyal to the God of Israel. This statement is confirmed in Chapter 3:18 where Daniel defied king Nebuchadnezzar when he stated, *"We want you know, O king, that we will not serve your gods or worship the image of gold you have set up."* Somehow God must have blinded the eyes of the Babylonian court officials as well as the king.

**It is important that we take a look at**

**Daniel 1:20**
> *20.    And in all matters of wisdom and understanding, that the king enquired of them, he found them ten times better that all the magicians and astrologers that were in all his realm.*

A cursory look at this verse could cause us to believe that Daniel and his friends were classed among the magicians and astrologers, both of which are an abomination to God.

A close look at the word syntax will reveal that the king was judging them in all matters of wisdom and understanding only, and NOT in the magical arts or astrology.

One can have knowledge but can lack wisdom and understanding. What the king was saying was that the magicians and astrologers did not compare with the Hebrew children when it came to the subjects of wisdom and understanding! Who knows? Maybe God caused king Nebuchadnezzar to exempt them from the subjects of Magic and Astrology!

God works in wonderful ways His wonders to perform! Elijah once thought that he was the only one left that was serving the Lord during the wicked reign of king Ahab and queen Jezebel.

Elijah moaned to God. *"The Israelites have rejected your covenant and broken down your altars, and put your prophets to death with the sword. I am the only one left, and now they are trying to kill me too."*

In verse 18 of 1 Kings Chapter 19, God gave this answer to Elijah, *"Yet I reserve seven thousand in Israel – all whose knees have not bowed down to Baal and all whose mouths have not kissed him."*

If you think you are the only Christian at your work, perhaps you should think again! Maybe God has someone  else He has reserved for Himself there that has not defiled themselves with the things of the world. This is one reason that we should never judge other people against ourselves. If you do, then you becomes like the Pharisee who openly derided the lowly sinner who beat his chest before God and said. "Forgive me Lord, for I am a sinner."

From the Scripture it is evident that somehow these four youngsters had managed, with God's help, and their own determination, to not defile themselves.

Just how determined are you and I in following Christ? Are we just "ja-broers" [one who agrees with everything, irrespective] or are we actively doing our best to be good citizens of the kingdom of God?

I recently saw a notice that reads as follows, "**God gives the nuts, but you have to crack them**."

If you do not try to do something yourself then God will not be able to help and guide you. If you are determined then, just like Daniel, you will have God's protection over you. God will keep you pure, even in a godless situation. What greater reward can you and I have?

### Daniel 2:1-19

*1.      And in the second year of the reign of Nebuchadnezzar Nebuchadnezzar dreamed dreams, wherein his spirit was troubled and his sleep brake from him*

*2.      Then the king commanded to call the magicians, and the astrologers, and the sorcerers, and the Chaldeans, for to shew the king his dreams. So they came and stood before the king.*

*3.      And the king said unto them, I have dreamed a dream, and my spirit was troubled to know the dream*

*4.      Then spake the Chaldeans to the king in Syriack, O king, live forever: tell thy servants the dream, and we will shew the interpretation.*

*5.    The king answered and said to the Chaldeans, The thing has gone from me: if you will not make known unto me the dream, with the interpretation thereof, ye shall be cut in pieces, and your  houses shall be made a dunghill.*

*6.    But if ye shew me the dream, and the interpretation thereof, ye shall receive of me gifts and rewards and great honour: therefore shew me the dream, and the interpretation thereof.*

*7.    They answered again and said, Let the king tell his servants the dream, and we shall shew the interpretation of it.*

*8.    The king answered and said, I know of certainty that ye would gain the time, because ye see the thing is gone from me.*

*9.    But if ye will not make known to me the dream, there is but one decree for you: for ye have prepared lying and corrupt words to speak before me, till the time be changed: therefore tell me the dream, and I shall know that ye can shew me the interpretation thereof.*

*10.    The Chaldeans answered before the king, and said, There is not a man upon earth that can shew the king's matter; therefore there is no king, lord, nor ruler, that asked such things at any magician, or astrologer, or Chaldean.*

*11.    And it a rare thing that the king requireth, and there is none other that can shew it before the king, except the gods, whose dwelling is not with flesh.*

*12.   For this cause the king was angry and very furious, and commanded to destroy all the wise men of Babylon.*

*13.   And the decree went forth that the wise men should be slain; and they sought Daniel and his fellows to be slain.*

*14.   Then Daniel answered with counsel and wisdom to Arioch the captain of the king's guard, which was gone forth to slay the wise men of Babylon.*

*15.   He answered and said to Arioch the king's captain, Why is the decree so hasty from the king? Then Arioch made the thing known to Daniel.*

*16.   Then Daniel went in, and desired of the king that he would give him time, and that he would shew the king the interpretation.*

*17.   Then Daniel went to his house, and made the thing known to Hananiah, Mishael, and Azariah, his companions:*

*18.   That they would desire mercies of the God of heaven concerning this secret; that Daniel and his fellows should not perish with the rest of the wise men of Babylon.*

*19.   Then was the secret revealed unto Daniel in a night vision. Then Daniel blessed the God of heaven*

After king Nebuchadnezzar had his dream of the wheat and the cows he called all his magicians, enchanters, sorcerers and astrologers together to tell him what he had dreamed. These were all the people God had warned long ago we were not to get involved with, not then, not now in our time, or ever. This warning still applies to the Christian today and will still apply in the future.

An interesting fact emerges out of this incident. Daniel and his three companions were not included in the group. A closer look at the Scriptures will reveal that the four were not classed under the magicians, etc, but were classed under the wise men only. One can be very wise without disobeying God's commands.

Because the king was very angry with the former group not being able to interpret his dream, he blindly gave the order to kill ALL his advisors, the innocent as well as the guilty.

Originally the king had ordered the execution of the astrologers only. Because the astrologers answered the king in a tactless way, they caused the king to become furious. It is often the case that the Christian suffers with the guilty. This happened to me many times, and no doubt will still happen again in the future. What counts is our attitude and our handling of the matter in tribulation.

You will notice that Daniel does not over-react or become angry. We should take his example. He exercised the gift of the Fruit of the Spirit in his life and actions. He acted with wisdom and tact, with the result that the lives of others were spared.

Verse 11 is also very interesting. Let's read it again: *"What the king asks is too difficult. No one can reveal it to the king except the gods, and they do not live among men."* Here we have their perception of the spiritual world. To most people God is so far away that they do not even believe God is near them. This is true of some Christians as well. If you think that God is far away from you, then certainly God can have no influence in your life.

Daniel, however, knew the living God and had a completely intimate relationship with Him. He knew that his God was near to him. In Jer. 33:3 God says: *"Call to me and I will answer you and tell you great and unsearchable things you do not know."* This was Daniel's secret, if you can call it that; this was his passport to success. If you take Daniel's example and live close to God and Jesus and the Holy Spirit you will surely be strengthened through ANY trial and tribulation you may go through during your lifetime. May God bless you as you put these words of wisdom into practice.

# CHAPTER 2

In the previous chapter we were at the place where king Nebuchadnezzar had blindly ordered the execution of all the wise men in Babylon, and that included Daniel and his companions even though they had not been with the astrologers and the magicians before the king when he had ordered them to tell him what he had dreamed and also to supply the interpretation of it. Daniel had asked an audience with the king so that he might ask for time to interpret the dream.

Daniel returned to his house and explained to his friends, Hananiah, Mishael and Azariah, what had happened.

This brings me to the first point:

# 1. Unity is Strength

**Daniel 2:17**

> 17    Then Daniel went to his house, and made the thing known to  Hananiah, Mishael, and Azariah, his companions.

Whenever you have a problem or something to share, do you share it with someone else; your partner, family or special friend? To share is to lighten one's burden. Paul, writing to the Philippian Church, had this to say to them: *"Yet it is good of you to share in my troubles. Moreover, as you Philippians know, in the early days of your acquaintance with the gospel, when I set out from Macedonia, not one church shared with me in the matter of giving and receiving, except you only; for even when I was in Thessalonica, you sent me aid again and again when I was in need. Not that I am looking for a gift, but I am looking for what may be credited to your account. I have received full payment and even more; I am amply supplied, now that I have received from Epaphroditus the gifts you sent. They are a fragrant offering, an acceptable sacrifice, pleasing to God. And my God will supply all your needs according to his riches in Christ Jesus. "(*Phil 4:14-19) (NIV)

In Gal. 6:2 Paul said: *"Carry each others burdens, and in this way you will fulfil the law of Christ."* Yet just a little further he had this to say: *"Each one should carry his own load."* This sounds like a contradiction, yet it is not! Paul is saying that no one should sponge on the other. And when each is truly carrying his own load, and along the way something happens then it is the duty of each one to help the other.

Daniel knew that to share his burden with others, with the right people, he would be strengthened. When a group of people with the same vision and the same goals in life get together to pray to the Lord, then powerful things will happen. The second point I would like to bring to you is God's action in this matter:

## 2. God's Action

**Daniel 2:18-19a**

*18      That they would desire mercies of the God of heaven concerning this secret; that Daniel and his fellows should not perish with the rest of the wise men of Babylon.*

*19a      Then was the secret revealed unto Daniel in a night vision.*

Jesus gave His disciples a very important piece of advice. We read in Matth 18:19 what He said: *"Again, I tell you that if two of you on earth agree about anything you ask for, it will be done for you by my Father in heaven. For where two or three come together in my name, there I am with them."*

Daniel was applying this principle when he asked his companions to plead with God for mercy in connection with the king's execution order. God honoured their sincere intentions not just because of their immediate prayer; but because their way of life was pleasing God. God does at times answer a sinner's prayer for something in his life, but God is not obliged to do so, as some seem to think. Many times God has said that His ear is not open to the asking of the wicked, except to one specific call only that of the request for salvation of the soul.

When your life is pleasing to the Lord, a sweet smelling sacrifice, then God's ear is open to your call for mercy, but not for your greediness. God answered Daniel's prayer in a strange way, by way of a vision. God answers our own prayers in ways that we do not expect. We may expect God to answer in a specific way or direction, yet He often gives the answer in quite another direction to which we expect it to be. When this happens we tend to ignore God, for the answer does not fit into OUR plans.

God's plans for us may be, and usually are quite different to what we expect it to be. Be open to the Holy Spirit and His leading. When we follow God's directions we will be blessed.

# 3. Daniel's reaction to the Vision

**Daniel 2:19b-23**

19b.   "........... Then Daniel blessed the God of heaven.

20.   Daniel answered and said, Blessed be the    name of God for ever and ever: for wisdom and might are his:

21.   And he changeth the times and the seasons: he removeth kings, and setteth up kings: he giveth wisdom unto the wise, and knowledge to them that know understanding:

22.   He revealeth the deep and secret things: he knoweth what is in the darkness, and the light dwelleth with him.

23.   I thank thee, and praise thee, O thou God of my fathers, who hast given me wisdom and might, and hast made known unto me now what we desired of thee: for thou hast now made known unto us the king's matter."

Daniel's reaction was spontaneous. He immediately praised the Lord his God. Do we thank the Lord when He answers our prayers and requests? I am afraid that we do not always give Him thanks, and I include myself in this. We receive a gift from God and we take it for granted; that it is our right to receive it. So often we pray for rain on a national basis, but when it rains, it is seldom that the nation gets down on its knees to thank God for His answering of our prayers. It has been done but very much fewer than the times asking.

We human beings tend to be a very ungrateful and unappreciative lot. Daniel praises God for who He is and what He is, the maker of the heaven and the earth, the all powerful One. Then he thanks God for the wisdom and the gifts God has given him. Notice one thing in Daniel's prayer of thanksgiving. Although God gave the interpretation of king Nebuchadnezzar's dream to him, Daniel included his companions in that thanksgiving. Daniel did not take the glory for himself. This shows that Daniel was a humble person. In verse 23 Daniel said: "I thank and praise you, O God of my fathers; You have given me wisdom and power, you have made known to me what we asked of you, you have made known to US [emphasis mine] the dream of the king."

We must always thank the Lord for all things in our lives. 1 Thess. 5:18 is very apt, and it reads as follows: *"In EVERYTHING [Emphasis mine] give thanks: for this is the will of God in Christ Jesus concerning you."* Put this into practice and you will be surprised just how your life will be improved and built up in Christ.

# 4. Daniel was a Man of Action

**Daniel 2:24-26**

> *24. Therefore Daniel went unto Arioch, whom the king had ordained to destroy the wise men of Babylon: he went and said thus unto him; Destroy not the wise men of Babylon: bring me in before the king. And I will show unto the king the interpretation.*
>
> *25. Then Arioch brought in Daniel before the king in haste, and said thus unto him, I have found a man of the captives of Judah, that will make known unto the king the interpretation.*
>
> *26. The king answered and said to Daniel, whose name was Belteshazer. Art thou able to make known unto me the dream which I have seen, and the interpretation thereof?*

Many Christians just sit and stagnate like a little pool of water gathering algae and mosquitoes. They just sit and wait for things to happen to them, and then wonder why God has not done a new thing in their life. Each person has to physically make an effort to put one foot in front of the other to enable him to get from one point to another. As I said previously; God gives the nuts, but you have to crack them! God helps those who help themselves.

Daniel did not let the flies gather on him. He went straight to the official Arioch and told him not to execute the wise men of Babylon. He also asked an audience with the king. That must have been early the following morning. When God tells us to do something we should act immediately.

Lastly we come to point No. 5.

## 5. Witnessing in the Face of Authority

**Daniel 2:27-28**

> 27.  *Daniel answered in the presence of the king, and said, The secret which the king hath demanded cannot the wise men, the astrologers, the magicians, the soothsayers, shew unto the king;*
> 28.  *But there is a God in heaven that revealeth secrets and maketh known to the king Nebuchadnezzar what shall be in the latter days.*

When asked if he could interpret the dream Daniel did not collect the honour for himself, but gave the glory to his God, the God of Abraham, Isaac and Jacob. I get very upset when I see billboards with captions that do not give Jesus the credit and that go something like this:

**Come and see Pastor X raise the dead, heal the sick and give sight to the blind. Be at such and such a place at such a time to see wonders performed!**

Jesus once said in Matth. 7:21-23: *"Not everyone who says to me, "Lord, Lord" will enter the kingdom of heaven, but only he who does the will of my Father who is in heaven. Many will say to me on that day, "Lord, Lord, did we not prophesy in your name and in your name drive out demons and perform miracles? Then I will tell them plainly, "I never knew you. away from me you evildoers!"*

Never take the glory for yourself when God gives you gifts to use in the assembly of the saints. This has been the downfall of some of the greatest of preachers. Daniel said: *"No wise man, enchanter, magician, or diviner can explain to the king the mystery he has asked about, but there is a God in heaven who reveals mysteries."* If Daniel can witness in the face of a great king, so can you and I witness to our bosses at work. You and I can only witness effectively when we witness in the power of the Holy Spirit.

We must remember that there is strength in unity, so never forsake the gathering of the saints: you cannot go it alone. When God speaks to you, don't delay, go into immediate action. Someone's life in eternity may depend on your response, and do not be afraid to witness at any time during your life. In season or out of season, and may God Bless you as you obey His instructions.

# CHAPTER 3

Daniel's life has much to say to us even in the stormy times we live in today. As we take a look at Daniel we will always be comparing his life to the way we should be living today, and how we can take an example from him. One thing I must strongly emphasize is that although we look at a human being for an example we must NEVER forget that Jesus is THE perfect and ultimate example.

Our eyes must never be taken off the Lord of lords, and the King of kings; for He is our guide through this life. The Holy Spirit glorifies Jesus, and it is the Holy Spirit that enlightens us to what is right and to what is wrong and sinful.

If you perhaps have a problem in differentiating between what is sin and what is pleasing to God, then may I venture to say that perhaps you are not born again of the Spirit. This has nothing to do with going to church and singing in the choir, etc. It has to do with a personal experience with, and commitment to, Jesus Himself. If you have not done so before, won't you take that very important step today?

## 1. The Acknowledgment of God's Greatness and Power.

**Daniel 2:46-47**

> *46. Then the king Nebuchadnezzar fell upon his face, and worshipped Daniel, and commanded that they should offer an oblation and sweet odours unto him.*
>
> *47. The king answered unto Daniel and said, of a truth it is, that your God is a God of gods, and the Lord of kings, and a revealer of secrets, seeing thou couldest reveal this secret.*

Daniel witnessed in the power of the Spirit before the face of king Nebuchadnezzar as to the greatness of his God, the living God. Daniel calls God the great God, the God above all gods, even above the Babylonian gods.

King Nebuchadnezzar humbled himself before Daniel by falling prostrate on the ground, acknowledging the greatness of Daniel's God through His servant Daniel. The words of the king: *"Surely your God is the God of gods and the Lord of the kings, and a revealer of mysteries for you were able to reveal this mystery,"* must also have had an impact on the other court officials that were present at the time.

It is worth examining verse 46, and certain words contained in it. On the surface it seems that the king started worshipping Daniel, as a god, and Daniel did nothing to stop it.

What does the word 'worship' really mean? It could mean several things; Apart from the worship of God, it also means: adore, reverence, esteem, to pay homage.

"Oblation" means sacrifice, offering, gift, present.

Now let us put that sentence in context. The real meaning of verse 46 should read something like this. Then king Nebuchadnezzar prostrated himself before Daniel in reverence and paid homage to him and ordered that the officials bring Daniels gifts and present, and to pour over Daniel expensive perfumes reserved only for the most important people.

It was (and in some places – still is ) the custom that whenever someone came into the presence of a person of higher position than himself that he bowed down, or prostrated himself before that person.

Now that that has been cleared up, let us continue further.

Your witnessing at work will also have an impact on others in the office. Negatively or positively, it WILL have an impact! Do not get discouraged when you witness and you find that those you witness to seem to be like a brick wall. Keep on praying, my Brother and Sister in the Lord, keep on praying through. Don't let the Devil get at you by discouraging you. Plant the seed of the Word in their hearts. Remember someone else will water and God will give the increase.

In my own case I was witnessed to as a young man of 19 yours old. I used to scoff at Terence Levey and laughed at his fervour for the Lord, yet, 23 years later, at the age of 42, I gave my life and heart to the Lord while on a business trip in the Transkei (South Africa). At the time of this publication I am 81 years old and still serving the Lord with fervour. This is why I say: Don't despair. Just keep on praying and witnessing for Jesus.

## 2. God's Reward

**Daniel 2:48-49**

*48.   Then the king made Daniel a great man, and gave him many great gifts, and made him ruler over the whole province of Babylon, and  chief of the governors over all the wise men of Babylon.*

*49.   Then Daniel requested of the king, and he set Shadrach, Meshach, and Abednego, over the affairs of the province of Babylon: but Daniel sat in the gate of the king.*

What happens when we faithfully keep on witnessing Jesus and His gospel to the world? God rewards his faithful servants! There is the well-known parable of Jesus about the talents.(Matth. 25:14-30)

What are we doing about the talents God has given us? Are we using them, or just ignoring them. When God sees that we are using the talents given us then He will add to these and give us even more authority in His Name. The rewards He gives us will not necessarily be great wealth and a very high position in the world. This may well be, but we must not covet money just for the sake of money. God will only reward you with wealth and position if He knows you will be able to handle it. If not, then He will reward you in other ways to suit what you will be able to handle.

True, God wants His children to have good health and enough to eat and drink and clothes to wear and to have a roof over our heads. The question is this: can you and I HANDLE what God gives us? God will not give you and I wealth or position if He knows that we are not able to carefully, and wisely, manage it.

God gives to us as our specific abilities develop. God wants us to grow in grace and in the truth of His Word. Great spiritual rewards await you and I when we follow the footsteps of Jesus. Therefore I plead with you not to be lax in witnessing Jesus to the world, not to be lax in your duty to your family, your work and to your country, no matter who is in power.

What can your greatest reward be? Let me take you back to the beginning of God's Word. In Genesis 15:1 God said to Abraham: *"Do not be afraid, Abram. I am your shield, your very great reward."* The very beginning of our spiritual and material growth can only start when we acknowledge God. Jesus and the Holy Spirit as an integral part of our lifestyle; not just for one hour a week on Sundays. This very great reward can be yours if you make Jesus Lord of your life

## 3. The Trials of the Believer

**Daniel 3:8-12**

> *8.    Wherefore at that time certain Chaldeans came near and accused the Jews.*

> *9.    They spake and said to the king Nebuchadnezzar; O king live, live for ever.*

> *10. Thou, O king hast made a decree, that every man that shall hear the sound of the cornet, flute, harp, sackbut, psaltery, and the dulcimer, and all kinds of music, shall fall down and worship the golden image;*

> *11. And who falleth not down and*

*worshippeth, that he should be cast into the midst of a burning fiery furnace.*

*12. There are certain Jews whom thou hast set over the affairs of the Province of Babylon, Shadrach, Meshach, and Abednego; these men, O king, have not regarded thee; they serve not thy gods, nor worship the golden image which thou hast set up.*

Jesus never said that the believer would live a life free of problems, as some preachers are apt to make us believe. In His Sermon on the Mount, Jesus spoke to His disciples in Matth. 5:10: *"Blessed are those who are persecuted because of righteousness, for theirs is the kingdom of heaven."* The apostle Paul, writing to Timothy, had this to say; "In fact, everyone who wants to live a godly life in Christ Jesus will be persecuted."

Persecution does not necessarily mean being thrown into Jail and receiving 49 lashes with the cat –'o-nine tails. It could mean being ignored at work and in the family. It could mean being sworn at, spat upon, and ostracized, etc. This was true in the case of Daniel and his friends. They had been wonderfully rewarded by the Lord at being placed at the court of the king, and they had the opportunity to witness to those around them by their lifestyle.

The way they conducted their lives in the way the Lord demanded from them are we also conducting our life the way the Lord demands of us?

Because of their exemplary conduct the other officials became very jealous, and the only way they could "get at them" was to find fault with their godly way of living. Try as they would, they could not find anything that dishonoured their position in the king's service. When you claim to be a child of God then your life immediately comes under microscopic scrutiny from the people of the world.

Make one mistake and it is thrown down your throat. Take Daniel's example and live a life of absolute purity. Do your best to be pure and fragrant in Jesus, and God will reward you abundantly.

## 4. The Christian "on the Carpet"

### Daniel 3:13-15

*13.    Then Nebuchadnezzar in his rage and fury commanded to bring Shadrach, Meshach and Abednego. Then they brought these men before the king.*

*14.    Nebuchadnezzar spake and said unto them, is it true, O Shadrach, Meshach, and Abednego, do ye not serve my gods, nor worship the golden image which I have set up?*

*15.    Now if ye be ready that at what time ye hear the sound of the comet, flute, harp, sackbut, psaltery, and dulcimer, and all*

*kinds of musick, ye fall down and worship the image which I have made; well: but if ye worship not, ye shall be cast the same hour into the midst*
*of a burning fiery furnace; and who is that god that shall deliver you out of my hands?*

In this instance it was the friends of Daniel who were out on the carpet for their so-called misconduct. Daniel was not with them at this time. He most probably was out in the provinces or perhaps acting as ambassador in another country. We do not know which. As previously mentioned, the Christian cannot go it alone. He is born-again into a very special family where love is to be one of the most important factors. On your own you are out of the love of the other members.

Because your own Christian life is affected by the other brothers and sisters, it is of vital importance to take Daniel's friends into account when looking at Daniel's lifestyle. They were summoned into the king's audience, probably forcibly, and king Nebuchadnezzar confronted them: *"Is it true Shadrach, Meshach and Abednego that you do not serve my gods or worship the image of gold I have set up?"* It could have been very easy for them to lie, but they stayed true to God. How would we fare in these circumstances?

# 5. No Apology Given

**Daniel 3:16-18**

*16. Shadrach, Meshach, and Abednego, answered and said to the king, O Nebuchadnezzar, we are not careful to answer thee in this matter.*

*17. If it be so, our God whom we serve is able to deliver us from burning fiery furnace and he will deliver us out of thine hand, O king.*

*18. But if not, be it known unto thee, O king, that we will not serve thy gods. Nor worship the golden image which you have set up.*

When the king gave them an ultimatum to bow down to the image their response was very implicit. They would NOT bow down to the golden image. Now study their reply very carefully, as we should apply this principle to our very own lives: *"O Nebuchadnezzar, we do not need to defend ourselves before you in this matter. If we are thrown into the blazing furnace, the God we serve is able to save us from it, and he will rescue us from your hand, O king."*

Here they show absolute confidence in God, but listen to the next verse, and note their unshakable attitude and loyalty to God: *"But even if he does not, we want you to know. O king, that we will not serve your gods or worship the image of gold you have set up."*

My brother and sister in Christ, THIS should be our aim and our goal in life, apart from the fact of serving Jesus. We need not be shaken up and formed into the mould of the world. If you have the armour of God, as mentioned in Ephesians chapter 5, and you use all of it, then you will be able to stand against the onslaughts of Satan. You do not need to apologize for the fact that you serve Jesus Christ. Be proud of it!

# CHAPTER 4

We come to a very interesting section of the book of Daniel. Although Daniel does not appear in this incident, I mentioned earlier that when we are in the company of born-again believers that live out the life of Jesus in the kingdom of God, we are greatly influenced by them Because these four men's lives were so closely intertwined, this incident has to be included in the lifestyle of Daniel.

To quickly sum up what had just happened to Shadrach, Meshach, and Abednego, as they were now called, they had just refused to bow down to the golden image.

High court intrigue had caused them to be brought before king Nebuchadnezzar. What these young men had said to the king infuriated him.

We need to take a very positive stand against the temptations of Satan. Many of Satan's temptations are very subtle and we should ask the Holy Spirit to reveal them to us. Many of us, even when they are revealed to us, tend not to believe that there is any demonic influence in them. The result – we disobey God! There are many temptations put in our path

Even while I was busy with this series over the CB (Citizen Band Radio) I went to our stationery department at work to buy some masking tape and other articles I needed for my studio at home. The lady behind the counter asked me why I was buying them instead of just booking them to the project I was working on, and then take them home, just like the others. When I told her that I do not work that way in my dealings, she suddenly became red in the face and made an excuse to get away. My brothers and sisters, be honest in ALL your dealings, even with the Receiver of Revenue.

## 1. The Change of Attitude and the Result

**Daniel 3:19-3**

>    19.   Then was Nebuchadnezzar full of fury, and the form of his visage was changed against Shadrwach, Meshach, and Abednego: therefore he spake and commanded that they should heat the furnace seven times more than is wont to be heated.

[also read verses 20 to 22]

*23.And these three men, Shadrach, Meshach, and Abednego, fell down*
*bound into the midst of the burning fiery furnace.*

As the lady in the stationery department had a change of attitude, so king Nebuchadnezzar had a change of attitude. The lady had an attitude of shame, but the king's attitude became vehement. I can just imagine the king's reaction as he shouted and ranted, when he brought down his wrath upon these young men.

Just after I became a true follower of Jesus and started to live out the Christian lifestyle, some of the staff at the place of my work changed their attitude towards me. I no longer went out with them on their drinking sessions; I no longer smoked. I stopped my swearing and cursing and all my dealings became honest dealings.

For three years I was persecuted to such an extent that they even tried their best to have me fired from the firm. To be able to do this they had to first find an excuse or something in my life or work that would give them a reason to do so. It is difficult for me to explain to you just how hard it was to work when you knew that many pairs of eyes were watching you every minute of the day.

Many times during each day I sent up arrow prayers to Jesus for wisdom, tact, and to amply supply me with the fruit of the Spirit. Through the Lord's help I was able to withstand the onslaught of Satan. Instead of complaining I accepted what the Lord had for me and through it I was strongly built up in faith. It would take too long to tell you all I went through, but be encouraged, if others can triumph through tribulation, then so can you!

These three young men accepted what the Lord had for them, even if they had to die for it. How strong is your faith? WE are to be overcomers; we are to overcome the temptations of the world. Not just one or two, but ALL the temptations. It CAN be done! I've been there, done that, got the T-shirt!

## 2. God's Protection.

**Daniel 3:24-26**

*24. Then Nebuchadnezzar was astonied* [astonished] *and rose up in haste, and spake, and said unto his counsellers. Did we not cast three men bound into the midst of the fire? They answered and said unto the king, True, O king.*

*25. He answered and said, Lo, I see four men loose walking in the midst of the fire, and they are not hurt; and the form of the fourth is like the Son of God.*

*26. The Nebuchadnezzar came near to the mouth of the burning fiery furnace, and spake, and said, Shadrach, Meshach, and Abednego, ye servants of the most high God, come forth, and come hither. Then Shadrach, Meshach, and Abednego, came forth of the midst of the fire.*

Shadrach, Meshach and Abednego were duly tied up and thrown into an extremely hot furnace. Many Christians have gone through great tribulation and many are undergoing great tribulation even today.

We sit comfortably in our own homes and are divorced from the true situation in many countries where Christians are persecuted, sometimes cruelly. No matter what the circumstances we find ourselves in, we should always rely on the Lord for His protection. God has never ever said that He will save us from physical persecution. If that were so, then many Christians have been beaten and maimed and killed for nothing.

Just read about the trials of Paul the Apostle, in 2 Cor. 11:16-33, and he was one of the most godly Christians that ever lived. No! God has only promised that Satan will never ever have authority over the soul of the believer who obeys God. Jesus once said: *"Do not be afraid of those who kill the body but cannot kill the soul."* (Matth. 10:28) Just remember one thing the destiny of your own body and soul is in your own hands.

Whatever decision you take depends on you, and only you can turn it into everlasting hell with Satan or to eternity with Jesus. The young men in the furnace knew this, and that they were safe in God's hands. Jesus is our protection, and his angels surround the believer.

God protected them while in the fire. King Nebuchadnezzar was amazed to see FOUR people in the fire; one more than had been thrown in. What was more, they were walking around in the furnace fire! Had the three not been firmly bound with ropes? Who was the fourth person? In the kings own words: "The fourth looks like a son of the gods."

What we have here is what is called in theological terms, a theophany – a manifestation or appearing of God to man. The person in the flames was none other than Jesus protecting His faithful followers. What is so significant here is that a heathen king did not call the fourth person a "god" but a "son of gods"

Jesus still helps and protects even today. Every day there are testimonies of God protecting his children. God does the same wonders today as He did then. Praise God, He is a living God!

## 3. A Miracle working God

**Daniel 3:27-28**

> *27. And the princes, governors, and captains, and the king's counsellers, being gathered together, saw these men, upon whose bodies the fire had no power, nor was*

*a hair of their head singed, neither were their coats changed, nor the smell of fire had passed on them.*

*28. Then Nebuchadnezzar spake, and said, Blessed be the God of Shadrach, Meshach, and Abednego, who hath sent his angel, and delivered his servants that trusted in him, and have changed the king's word, and yielded their bodies, that they might not serve and worship any god, except their own God.*

It is a very sad thing that there are beautiful Christians who flatly refuse to believe that God is a living God as far as miracles is concerned and that the full working of the Holy Spirit is not for today. Jesus is the same yesterday, the same today and will be the same tomorrow right into eternity. King Nebuchadnezzar now recognizes that these Hebrew young men serve the Most High God. This is the second encounter he has had with the God of Abraham, Isaac and Jacob.

Many have had a second encounter with God, yet a short while later, we seem to pass it by as if it, were just a worldly happening. Satan often blinds the eyes of Christians who are not strong enough in the faith.

Here the king sees the young men come out of the fire with not even their hair singed, clothes burnt and not even the smell of fire on them and this must have had quite an impression on all watching these proceedings. Depending on the occasion, God does things in small ways, as well as other times in an impressive way. This surely was very impressive, as God demonstrated to all the officials of a very powerful nation that He was even greater than them and all their magicians.

In Nebuchadnezzar's second encounter with God he again praises God and acknowledges that God sent His Angel to protect them. Notice also that he equates the son of a god with an angel of the Lord. After this incident we do not hear of these three again during the period of Daniel.

## 4. Nebuchadnezzar's Decree

**Daniel 3:29-30**

> 29. *Therefore I make a decree, that every people , nation, and language which speak anything amiss against the God of Shadrach, Meshach, and Abednego, shall be cut in pieces, and their houses shall be made a dunghill; because there is no other God that can deliver after this sort.*

> 30. *Then the king promoted Shadrach, Meshach, and Abednego, in the province of Babylon.*

The king does something that other kings and leaders of countries have copied again and again. Yet in this we have a very serious warning. I wonder if you can pick it up?

The Roman emperor Constantine, who reigned during the years 306 to 337 AD, established Christianity as the official religion of the country. He was alleged to have had a vision of Christ who said to him that if he followed Him he would be given wealth and position. One minute he was killing the Christians and the next moment it was the heathens turn to be persecuted.

True Christianity cannot be forced on people. No one can be forced into the kingdom of God. It has to be through the proper gateway, and that through Christ Himself. Many people kid themselves that they are candidates for heaven while they are in fact far away from Jesus. Many walk next to Jesus, yet do not have Jesus in their heart. They too are going to be disappointed. Unfortunately many have been deceived into this position.

Those of you reading this book should by now know the conditions of entering everlasting life with Christ. I invite you to come to Jesus and take Him into your life, and if you already have, then rededicate yourself to His service.

# CHAPTER 5

We have just handled Nebuchadnezzar's second encounter with Daniel's God in the incident of the golden image he set up in Babylon. You may remember that all three the young men had refused to bow down to the image and, because of jealousy, the other court officials reported this fact to the king. The three were subsequently bound and thrown into the fiery furnace. They survived, through the help of God's Angel, who was none other than Jesus, the fourth person in the furnace. Because of this miracle the king declared that anyone speaking against the God that the Hebrews served would be put to death, and their property destroyed.

# 1. The King's Witness, his Problem, and his third Encounter with God.

**Daniel 4:1-9**

*1. Nebuchadnezzar the king, unto all people, nations, and languages, that dwell in all the earth; Peace be multiplied unto you.*

*2. I thought it good to shew the signs and wonders that the high God hath wrought toward me.*

*3. How great are his signs! And how mighty are his wonders! His kingdom is an everlasting kingdom, and his dominion is from generation to generation.*

*4. I Nebuchadnezzar was at rest in mine house, and flourishing in my palace:*

*5. I saw a dream which made me afraid, and the thoughts upon my bed and the visions of my head troubled me.*

*6. Therefore made I a decree to bring in all the wise men of Babylon before me, that they might make known unto me the interpretation of the dream.*

*7. Then came in the magicians, the astrologers, the Chaldeans, and the soothsayers: and I told the dream before them; but they did not make known unto me the interpretation thereof.*

*8. But at the last Daniel came before me, whose name was Belteshazzar, according to the names of my god, and in whom is the spirit of the holy gods: and before him I told the dream, saying,*

*9. O Belteshazzar, master of the magicians, because I know that the spirit of the holy gods is in thee, and no secret toubleth thee, tell me the visions of my dream that I have seen, and the interpretation thereof.*

We came now to the later time in Daniel's stay in exile in Babylon. I suspect that by now they were not the very young men we have been studying. The king had another dream and although he knew that Daniel had been instrumental in interpreting the previous one in a most wonderful way, for some reason Daniel was not called in, even though he was appointed over all the wise men in Babylon. Notice that these men had been reinstated to their previous positions in the province of Babylon.

Once again Daniel was not with the wise men before the king. Only when all the other wise men in the form of magicians, astrologers, etc. could not interpret the dream was Daniel called into the picture. I personally believe that God had kept Daniel away on business so that once again He may reveal to the king and his court officials His power and His glory to the heathens through His servant Daniel.

Have you often wondered just why others get the best jobs and you do not? I put it to you that maybe God is doing that on purpose so that His purpose may be fulfilled in you completely, another way, even better than you could have hoped it to be. Paul, through the Spirit, told the slaves to be content in where they are, for in doing so they will be a witness to the working of God and the Holy Spirit in their lives. In other words, they will be acting quite differently to the moaning and groaning and complaining of the other slaves. Their lifestyle would reflect the peace of God in their hearts.

Be content with what you have. When you have this peace in your life then God can do something with you because now you are in God's will and not your will against the will of God.

King Nebuchadnezzar witnessed in a wonderful way of God's goodness and His power. He wrote a letter to all the people around him, including all the nations. Today we are more and more seeing people on the Television giving their witness as to how Jesus helps them in many things. This is another way of witnessing to the nations.

Notice that the king was at home, contented and prosperous. Now God comes along and shatters his peace with another dream. The moment one becomes complacent or completely satisfied with life in general that is when the danger signs appear. This is the time that we have to be aware of our slowly slipping back into the world. The Israelites slipped into idolatry and away from God exactly the time they were prosperous and contented. Only when they were in such dire straits and deep in trouble with the world did they come to call on

Jehovah their God. How often one calls upon God and no answer is forthcoming from Him because we call on Him in our pride, or greed or even with wrong motives. Only when our life is committed to Jesus is He obliged to answer us. Christ said that only if we abide in Him and He abides in us will our prayers be answered. Is THIS the reason perhaps why your prayers are never answered?

Why is it that God shatters our lives sometimes? Many preachers say that because God is a God of love He will never allow anything to happen to the believer. Don't believe this at all. The Scriptures tell me another story! It is because of his love that He sometimes has to turn us upside down and spank our bottoms so that we may know that we have to come back in line with His will and wishes.

Let us go now to verse 18 and continue from there.

## 2. The king acknowledges Daniels God-given Authority

**Daniel 4:18**

> 18. This dream I king Nebuchadnezzar have seen. Now thou, O Belteshazzar, declare the interpretation thereof, foremost as all the wise men of my kingdom are not able to make known unto me the interpretation: but thou art able; for the spirit of the holy gods is in thee.

In this third encounter with God, Nebuchadnezzar, who for seven years had been a madman eating grass and sleeping in the open because he had been too proud to acknowledge God as the only living God, whom he had worshipped, recognized that the interpretation had indeed been true and trustworthy. Finally he recognized that God was working through His servant Daniel for the good of the country, so that God may be glorified.

You may be witnessing for Jesus now for many years without anyone really giving you recognition for what you have or are doing. You wonder just why you get overlooked for the eldership, the deaconship or any other of the leadership positions in your congregation. Don't despair, just carry on doing the Lord's work, not for your own glory, but for the glory of the Lord.

When the Lord sees that you can handle His work in a humble fashion without receiving the glory for yourself, He will send you up the ladder. Be warned, however, the moment you try to receive the glory for yourself, your fall will be great. The higher up the ladder of successful working for the Lord, the greater will be your fall. In all your dealings rely totally upon the Holy Spirit.

A great book to read is the life of the late Pastor Duma called, **"Take your Glory Lord."** It is well worth reading and it will enrich your own life. [South Africa]

# 3. Daniel's Perplexity

**Daniel 4:19**

> *19.        Then Daniel whose name was Belteshazzar, was astonied (astonished) for one hour, and his thoughts troubled him. The king spake, and said, Belteshazzar, let not the dream, or the interpretation thereof, trouble thee. Belteshazzar answered and said, My Lord, the dream be to them that hate thee, and the interpretation thereof to thine enemies.*

Daniel received the interpretation of the king's dream and in it he saw that the king was in for a hard time ahead if he did not listen to the warning of the Lord. He knew the king fairly well by this time to know that the king would not heed God's message to him. The king recognized that the message would not be a pleasant one, yet he told Daniel not to be worried about it. Daniel's expression of the face must have been very plain. Normally to have that type of facial expression in the presence of the king would have resulted in him being put to death. Indeed Daniel was in a favoured position with the king by this time.

Daniel went ahead and told the king the interpretation of the dream. When God gives you or I a message for someone, we often are afraid to go ahead with the instruction.

I personally have failed the Lord many times in this respect, and I am not proud of it. Yet when we take the step forward in faith we become surprised at the outcome. Why? Because when we go out in faith, the Holy Spirit is ahead of us preparing the way. God works in the most wonderful ways. Praise His Holy Name!

## 4. Daniel's godly Advice

**Daniel 4:26-27**

> 26. And whereas they commanded to leave the stump of the tree roots; thy kingdom will be sure unto thee, after that thou shalt have known that the heavens do rule.
>
> 27. Where, O king, let my counsel be acceptable unto thee, and break off thy sins by righteous, and thine iniquities by shewing mercy to the poor, if it may be a lengthening of thy tranquility.

"The command to leave the stump of the tree with its roots means that your kingdom will be restored to you when you acknowledge that Heaven rules. Therefore. O king, be pleased to accept my advice: Renounce your sins by doing what is right, and your wickedness by being kind to the oppressed. It may be that then your prosperity will continue."

Unfortunately, as with so many of us today, the king did not heed God's word to him. Why is it that so many have to first fall into the fire and roast before they listen? It is like putting up a "Wet Paint" sign. You can be sure you will find many sets of fingerprints as a testimony that people have not believed the sign, only to find that it was true.

God's word is ever true. Don't fall into the fire; come to Jesus before that happens. In verse 34 Nebuchadnezzar said: *"At the end of that time, I Nebuchadnezzar, raised my eyes toward heaven, and my sanity was restored. Then I praised the Most High; I honoured and glorified him who lives forever."* We see here Daniel's godly influence, years later, over others and the king. May our godly living influence others in our own part of God's vineyard

As far as we know, king Nebuchadnezzar honoured God for the rest of his life. How about you? Has Daniel spoken to you, and brought the gospel to you, and have you refused it?

I pray that you will become like the king who eventually received his salvation. Do it now! Tomorrow may be too late!

# CHAPTER 6

## *Daniel during the Reign of king Belshazzar*

U p to the end of chapter 4 we were in the period of king Nebuchadnezzar and he had to have three encounters with the power and glory of the living God before he eventually resigned himself into God's care.

That was the end of one kingly reign, and now we come into another kingly reign; that of his son Belshazzar. In fact, his reign began at the beginning of the crumbling of the Babylonian Empire.

Let us look what Belshazzar's name means.
It means: May the god Bel protect the king or the lord's leader.
[the word "lord" with a small letter "l"]

Nebuchadnezzar gave this name to his son thinking

that this son would one day protect him in later life through the help of the Babylonian god Bel, the god of the earth. Does this ring a bell somewhere if I may be permitted a pun? Satan is called the god of the earth and one of his names is Belial, the spirit of evil personified.

Here Belshazzar has given himself over into the hands of the god Bel. Satan truly had taken over Belshazzar's life and he was determined to bring it into ruin. Satan still does that today by deceiving the unsuspecting into a life away from Christ. This brings us to the first point.

## 1. Belshazzar the Extravagant

**Daniel 5:1**

> 1. *Belshazzar made a great feast to a thousand of his lords, and drank wine before the thousand.*

Belshazzar, in the giving of this very extravagant party, followed somewhat in the footsteps of his father. Nebuchadnezzar had been proud of his wealth and his authority and the way he had handled it. In the end he humbled himself before God to such an extent that after he had acknowledged God as his Most High God, he was restored to a position wealth. Why? He now knew how to handle his wealth. Now here comes his son, and starts to squander what his father had carefully built up. Is it not amazing that when one person gathers with a lot of hard work, another comes and throws it to the wind in a passion of disconcern.

There is a very good Afrikaans expression that sums all this up; "Erfgeld is swerfgeld". [loosely tanslated – Inheritance money is drifting or travel money]

Belshazzar, in total disregard to the economy of the state, and his country, gives this huge drunken orgy. We must take this as a lesson for ourselves. Be careful with that which God gives us. If you have already committed yourself to Jesus then everything you have belongs to God, and if you do not manage it like a faithful steward should, then God may just take it away from you, and give it to someone else who IS able to manage it properly. Jesus gave a few parables to illustrate this very point.

Another point that comes out of this act is that it is dangerous to live off the glory of others.

## 2. The Desecration of God's Belongings

**Daniel 5:2-4**

> *2.   Belshazzar, whiles he tasted the wine, commanded to bring the golden and silver vessels which his father Nebuchadnezzar had taken out of the temple which was in*

*Jerusalem; that the king, and his princes, his wives and his concubines, might drink therein.*

*3. Then they brought the golden vessels that were taken out of the temple of the house of God which was at Jerusalem; and the king, and his princes, and his wives, and concubines, drank in them*

*4. They drank wine, and praised the gods of gold, and of silver, of brass, of iron of wood, and of stone.*

One thing about Nebuchadnezzar was that the golden articles taken from the temple in Jerusalem went straight into his treasury, and stayed there. He never took them out to use them. When one inherits wealth there is the desire to show off and to spend it on luxuries. It looks like that happened to Belshazzar, as he gave a great banquet for a thousand of his nobles. Babylon was well known for its hanging gardens and luxury and wickedness.

Many of the satanic religions emanated from this city. The religions that started here often seem to be moving toward God, yet they do the opposite as they cause worshippers to move away from the true living God Jehovah and His Son Jesus Christ.

Nimrod, Semiramis, Tammuz, and the goddess Astaroth or Isthar, were all part of Babylon. From the goddess Ishtar we have the derived name of Easter. She was the chief goddess and her worship was marked by sexual orgies and rites. Theologically the word Easter should never be part of the

Christian's vocabulary. In Egypt, the name for the goddess Isthar was Isus or Horus, and from there the practice of the horoscope, the reading of one's fortune from the stars, an abomination to the Lord. Belshazzar was in the middle of all this evil influence.

Daniel was sent by God right into the middle into this den of wickedness to testify of his God Jehovah. Do you sometimes feel that you are in a den of iniquity at work? Maybe God has sent you there to be a shining light for Him, so that you may reveal God's glory to them! If you are in that position, then stay there until God releases you into another area. God will give you the strength to endure.

Back to Belshazzar's party:
When the Christian starts to slowly return to the ways of the world, he starts to desecrate the things of God, especially the name of God, Jesus and the Holy Spirit. Blasphemy against the Holy Spirit is not tolerated by God. The death of Ananias and Saphira is one example (Acts 5:1-11) Here Belshazzar certainly blasphemed to the utmost and God had something to say to him, and this brings us to God's action and reaction.

# 3. God's Reaction

**Daniel 5:5-6**

> *5. In the same hour came forth fingers of a*

*man's hand, and wrote over against the candlestick upon the plaister of the wall of the king's palace; and the king saw the part of the hand that wrote.*

*6. Then the king's countenance was changed, and his thoughts troubled him, so that the joints of his loins were loosed, and his knees smote one against another.*

*"Suddenly the fingers of a human hand appeared and wrote on the plaster of the wall, near the lampstand in the royal palace. The king watched the hand as it wrote. His face turned pale and he was frightened that his knees knocked together and his legs gave way." (NIV)*

This was not just a ghostly hand that wrote on the wall but a human hand, a hand of blood and flesh, and it must have been a very frightening experience. God made sure that everyone would see that hand and the writing by performing this miracle at the main point of illumination. The light of the oil lamps reflecting off the moving hand drew everyone's attention to it. God made sure that it could not be missed! The king, in his drunken state, knew immediately that it was meant for him, even though he did not understand the message.

Although maybe not so dramatically, God even today visibly opens and closes doors to everyone. It is for us to see and take note. We see, but don't understand when we are not following God close enough. Whenever we see, we do not ask His advice.

Instead of going down on our knees and asking God what to do next, we go on in our own strength, and we fail miserably. We forget to call on God, and we suffer the consequences thereof.

## 4. Belshazzar Calls for Help

**Daniel 5:7-9**

> *7. The king cried aloud to bring in the astrologers, the Chaldeans, and the soothsayers. And the king spake, and said to the wise men of Babylon, whosoever shall read this writing, and shew me the interpretation thereof, shall be clothed with scarlet, and have a chain of gold about his neck, and shall be third ruler in the kingdom.*
>
> *8. Then came in all the king's wise men; but they could not read the writing, nor make known to the king the interpretation thereof.*
>
> *9. Then was king Belshazzar greatly troubled, and his countenance was changed in him, and his lords were astonied* [astonished].

Verse 7 says: *"The king called out for the enchanters, astrologers and diviners to be brought."* Remember this is while he is lying flat out on the floor of the banquet room with a thousand people around him. Verse 8 said that his legs had given away under him. Belshazzar was not ignorant of Jehovah, the

91

God of Daniel, because he had been brought up and trained in the court of his father Nebuchadnezzar and had seen his father while he was a madman, and after that when God had restored him to his throne again.

There is no excuse for us on that day when God calls us all before the great white throne in judgment, the believers in Jesus for their works, or the works they did not do, and the unbelievers to everlasting damnation for not accepting Jesus as their Saviour. Hard words, but these are God's, not mine. Read the Scriptures for confirmation. Belshazzar called the wrong people in. He should have called on the writer of the message – God.

Once again Daniel was not among the magicians! It seems as if Belshazzar had removed Daniel from office and had forgotten about him.

## 5. God's Messenger

**Daniel 5:10-12**

> 10.     Now the queen, by reason of the words of the king and his lords, came into the banquet house; and the queen spake and said, O king, live forever: let not thy thoughts trouble thee, nor let thy countenance be changed.
>
> 11.     There is a man in thy kingdom, in whom is the spirit of the holy gods; and in the day of thy father light and

*understanding and wisdom, like the wisdom of the gods, was found in him; whom the king Nebuchadnezzar thy father, the king, I say, thy father, made master of the magicians, astrologers, Chaldeans, and sooths*

*12.   Forasmuch as an excellent spirit and knowledge, and understanding, interpreting of dreams, and shewing of hard sentences, and dissolving of doubts, were found in the same Daniel, whom the king named Belteshazzar; now let Daniel be called, and he will shew the interpretation.*

Wives are so often taken for granted and some seem to think that they must not mingle in the household affairs or know anything about the finances. How wrong can we be! Here in the most difficult time of his life comes his wife, the queen, and gives him some very good advice. He has no option but to take it. All of this would not have been necessary if he had but heeded his father and followed in his father's footsteps as far as the ways of Jehovah was concerned.  He had the knowledge, but he did not use it

What are you and I doing with the knowledge we get from the messages we receive from our own pastors or priests? Do you just listen, and say; "What a beautiful message!" and to go on and do the things you are not supposed to do? May each of us go out today with the resolution, that from now on, we are going to be doers of the Word and not just listeners.

Daniel was not just a listener, he certainly was a doer, and that is why God blessed him even in his position of an exile in a godless society.

May God bless us as we go out and be doers of the Word!

# CHAPTER 7

**Daniel 5:13-17**

13.       *Then was Daniel brought in before the king. And the king spake and said unto Daniel. Art thou that Daniel, which art of the children of Judah, whom the king my father brought out of Jewry?*

14.       *I have even heard of thee, that the spirit of the gods is in thee, and that light and understanding and excellent wisdom is found in thee.*

15.       *And now the wise men, and astrologers, have been brought in before me, that they should read this writing, and make known unto me the interpretation thereof: but they could not shew me the interpretation of the thing;*

16.       *And I have heard of thee, that thou canst make interpretations, and dissolve doubts: now if thou canst read the writing, and make known to me the interpretation thereof, thou shalt be clothed with scarlet, and have a chain of gold about thy neck, and shalt be third ruler in the*

*kingdom.*

*17.     Then Daniel answered and said before the king. Let thy gifts be to thyself, and give thy rewards to another; yet I will read the writing unto the king, and make known to him the interpretation.*

Nebuchadnezzar was no longer king of Babylon, and his son Belshazzar was now sitting on the throne, living it up like it was going out of fashion. He was in the middle of a massive party he had thrown for a thousand of his officials. It was a very extravagant one, thrown no doubt to impress others of the wealth he had inherited from his father.

In his drunkenness he had called for the golden cups, etc, captured from the temple in Jerusalem years earlier. He desecrated them in an ungodly manner by drinking wine out of them in a den of wickedness. This brought the wrath of God down upon him.

Suddenly a hand appears and the fingers write on the wall near the royal lampstand. Belshazzar got such a fright that his legs buckled from underneath him and as he lay on the floor he called for help from his so-called wise men. They could not help him. His wife, the queen, came to his rescue by asking him to call Daniel to interpret the writing.

What we learn from this incident as applied to our lives and for ourselves is that we are not to desecrate the inheritance we have received as a son and daughter of God in His kingdom. Rev. 21:7 says *"He that over cometh shall inherit all things, and I will be his God, and he shall be my son."* Take time to study the Scriptures to find out just how much you and I have inherited from the Father.

# 1. King Belshazzar's Apparent Ignorance
## (vs 13-15)

*"Are you Daniel, one of the exiles my father the king brought from Judah?"* Although he said this, Belshazzar was not ignorant of Daniel. I mentioned in the previous chapter that Belshazzar had been brought up and taught in the court of his father king Nebuchadnezzar. It appears that he had years earlier relieved Daniel of his post after the death of his father, and that he no longer was ruler over the province of Babylon.

It is a sad occasion when the children of godly parents do not follow in their footsteps in serving the Living God. They see first hand the blessings of the Lord and what He is able to do in their lives, yet they choose to ignore what they see and hear. Satan's temptations in the world have lured them to him. This is true even in my own household. Only one of my three children is serving the Lord. I am sure there are many of you that have this same heartache. Please, never weary of praying for their release from darkness in to the salvation light of

Jesus Christ.

Belshazzar, at the time of this party, had all but forgotten about Daniel, and here in his drunken state had forgotten about him completely. Here is a warning for us; Paul said to the Ephesians in Eph 5:15-18, *"Be very careful, then, how you live – not as unwise but as wise, making the most of every opportunity, because the days are evil. Therefore do not be foolish, but understand what the Lord's will is. Do not get drunk on wine, which leads to debauchery. Instead, be filled with the Spirit."*

Drunken parties leads to all kinds of evil, so let us be careful of the company we keep!

## 2. Daniel offered a Reward (vs 16)

*"If you can read this writing and tell me what it means, you will be clothed in purple and have a gold chain placed around your neck, and you will be made the third highest ruler in the kingdom."* The king told Daniel.

How often the world offers rewards to people to get something out of them. This type of attitude more than often breeds another type of attitude, even worse than the first – an attitude of "pay me first and then I will tell you, or do it!" – a type of bribe if you want to call it that. Does your child tell you that he will not cut the grass, or anything else for that matter, unless you pay him for doing it? If you fall for that trap then you have only yourself to blame.

Certainly certain jobs around the house can be paid jobs so that he knows that he has earned his pocket money. Odd jobs can also be given him so that he may earn a little bit extra, BUT, and a big BUT, he must also know that there is such a thing as authority in the house which must be obeyed without question and without payment.

Did you know that in our spiritual life we also have to do a lot of things for the Lord without payment, or looking for rewards. In fact, we should not even expect to be "Paid" for it. Why? Slaves normally only receive their food and clothing as needed, with very little to spend for themselves.

Are we not slaves unto the Lord Jesus; voluntarily and out of LOVE for Him? Are you truly a servant and a slave to Jesus? Be a slave and a servant of Jesus and then, and only then, will you receive everlasting rewards that will not perish or rust.

## 3. Daniel's answer.

Daniel's reaction to the king's offer of reward was short and sweet: *"You may keep your gifts for yourself and give your rewards to someone else."* Here he is given the offer of a lifetime, which most people would kill for, and he pushes it aside! What would you do? Whenever raffles or such like come around the office and I am approached, I do not partake in them, except perhaps just to note it down as a donation if the occasion warrants it. Most people just don't understand my attitude.

Quite a few years ago there was a completion on the go for a Million Rand win and the tickets were sold for R10. I was approached, and as some of the money was going to charity. I took a ticket and just wrote Donation in the place where my name should have been. I did not even bother to take the counterslip. When the person kept on insisting that I take it as I may possibly be the winner of a million rand, to please him I took the counterslip, and as I tore it up I thought he was going to have a heart attack

The Christian should not be caught up in the money race. It is impossible to serve money and the Lord at the same time, so be careful how you work with money. Daniel did not let money go to his head. He was totally committed to God, and did not let money, or wealth interfere with his worship of the Lord. It was not for nothing that Jesus said in Matth 6:24: *"You cannot serve both God and money,"* or as the KJV puts it; *"Ye cannot serve God and mammon."* Mammon being the Aramaic word for riches; which, in turn means money.

# 4. Daniel Obeys in all Circumstances

Daniel certainly was a steadfast man, for by now he was a grown-up man. He never budged an inch from what he had set himself to do, and that was to never let his God down in ANY circumstance. He had what one would call today a "one-track mind" as far as serving his God was concerned.

We should be like that. He was not ashamed of his God as many are of Jesus today. It amazes me that so many Christians are afraid to let others know who they stand for and when confronted many are very apologetic over their relationship with Christ.

I have a fish sign on my car and I am proud of it. There is one drawback to this – one has to be very careful how you drive and act, as all eyes are on you now. I have seen many a car with the fish sticker on it do the most dangerous and irresponsible driving.

Before I retired I had a fish sticker on my cabinets, at work and another that advertised Jesus as my Guide. I was leader of a twice-weekly Christian group that held meetings during lunch hour. We had people coming from other firms to attend our meetings. Most of the Black people at work called me Umfundisi, which means teacher or preacher in the Zulu language.

May I challenge you to go out and advertise that you are a slave of Jesus; that He is your Saviour, and then don't let Jesus be ashamed of you as you do your very best to live out the Christian life to the full. Ask the Holy Spirit to help and guide you. Should you fall, don't just lie there; get up, dust yourself off by asking God's forgiveness and carry on walking in God's light.

Remember, Daniel was flesh and blood just like you and I. If he could do it, then certainly the potential is in each of us to do the same.

Next we will examine the actual interpretation of the message on the wall.

# CHAPTER 8

## *Summary about Belshazzar so far.*

King Belshazzar was at the extravagant party he gave at the royal palace and how he had called for the golden gobbles or cups to be brought out of the treasury, so that they could drink out of them. Unfortunately for him he called for the articles that had been taken out of the temple at Jerusalem.

We learnt that God does not tolerate any desecration of what is His, and how we are to look after our own bodies that are the temple of God if we are born-again of the Spirit and have Jesus as our Saviour.

While he was still drinking out of one of the cups, God sent a human hand which wrote on the wall near the candlestick. His wise men could not interpret the writing so, on behalf of his wife, the queen, he sent for Daniel. Verse 17 told of Daniel's answer.

We take it up again where Daniel obeyed despite his dislike for the king. At work we are also to obey the authority we have put ourselves under. Remember, YOU contracted yourself to the work you are in at the present and as such put yourself under the authority of your employers. Daniel had no choice. He was still a "prisoner" in Babylon.

**Daniel 5:18-24**

18.      *O thou king, the most high God gave Nebuchadnezzar thy father a kingdom, and majesty, and glory, and honour.*

19.      *And for the majesty that he gave him, all people, nations, and languages, trembled and feared before him: and whom he would he slew; and whom he would he kept alive; and whom he would he put down.*

20.      *But when his heart was lifted up, and his mind hardened in pride, he was deposed from his kingly throne, and they took his glory from him:*

21.      *And he was driven from the sons of men; and his heart was made like the beasts, and his dwelling was with the dew of heaven; till he knew that the most high God ruled in the kingdom of men, and that he appointeth over it whomsoever he will.*

22.      *And thou his son, O Belshazzar, hast not humbled thine heart, though thou knewest all this;*

23.      *But has lifted up thyself against*

*the Lord of heaven; and they have brought the vessels of his house before thee, and thou, and the lords, thy wives, and thy concubines, have drunk wine in them, and thou hast praised the gods of silver, and gold, of brass, iron, wood and stone, which see not, nor hear, nor know,; and the God in whose hand thy breath is, and whose are all the ways, hast thou not glorified:*

*24.        Then was the part of the hand sent from him; and this writing was written.*

The interpretation of the message is actually three-fold:

## 1. The Message was Given to Belshazzar

The interpretation was immediate as Belshazzar was still at the party with all his officials around him. The message was directed to him as he, being the ruler of the empire, was the responsible person. He should have been an example to his officials and to his subjects in the empire. Daniel reminded Belshazzar that God was the one who should have been his example.

In verse 19 he told the king: *"Because of the high position he* (God) *gave him* (Nebuchadnezzar), *all the peoples and nations and men of every language dreaded and feared him."* Immediately after saying this Daniel confronted the king with the following statement: *"But you his son, O Belshazzar, have not humbled yourself, though you knew all this."*

How often we know from the Scriptures, that we have to behave in a certain manner as a Christian, but we choose to ignore what Jesus says to us in His Word. We have the Spirit in us telling us not to do or say a certain thing, yet we rebel and do as we please, knowing that God is not going to approve, and also that we will be punished for disobeying.

One cannot sin and get away from the punishment. If anyone reading this is wilfully sinning against the Lord, won't you make right with Jesus right now, even while reading this book. Don't put it off until later, because later will be too late, and then you will have missed the opportunity God has given you right now.

God spoke to Belshazzar directly, as an individual, just as He is talking to you right now, through this message. Please do not let the indictment (aanklag) be against you, that you, like the king, you have set yourself up against the Lord of heaven.

## 2. The Message was to the Officials

The second part of the interpretations was towards the officials in the company of Belshazzar. They also should have known better. They too were in a rulership position and should have taken a stand. True, it could have cost them their life opposing the king, but Jesus once said that it would be better to lose one's life than to lose the salvation of the soul.

When it comes to us today, how do we act in the presence of our superiors? Do we take a stand when we see that we are being expected to take part in some shady deal or something that will be underhand and contrary to God's Word?

Do you and I take stand and show our true colours in the Lord Jesus? It is hard to do, but Jesus expects us to do just that, even at the cost of being fired from our job. When that happens, the Lord will look after you and me when we ask Him for help. If the Lord looks after the lilies of the field and the sparrow, how much more will He not look after His children.

More often than not, you will find that after you have taken your stand, your superiors and your colleagues will respect you, even if they do not openly show it.

## 3. The Message was for the People in General at that Time.

### (The Writing and the Message was also for People of all Ages)

The writing on the wall was in three sections, the first and last of which can be lumped into one as they form a unit. It is the middle section that we will be examining now, as this is the crux of the message. The first and the last being the introduction and the conclusion of the message.

Verse 27 is the thrust of the message to king Belshazzar.

## Daniel 5:25-31

> 25.    And this is the writing that was written: ME-NE, ME-NE, TE-KEL, U-PHAR-SIN.
> 26.    This is the interpretation of the thing; ME-NE; God hath numbered thy kingdom, and finished it.
> 27.    TE-KE; Thou art weighed in the balance, and art found wanting.
> 28.    PE-RES; Thy kingdom is divided, and given to the Medes and the Persians.
> 29. Then commanded Belshazzar and they clothed Daniel with scarlet, and put a chain of gold about his neck, and made a proclamation concerning him, that he should be the third ruler in the kingdom.
> 30.    In that night was Belshazzar the king of the Chaldeans slain.
> 31. And Darius the Median took the kingdom, being about three score and two years old.

Let us do a bit of exegesis on verse 27. Exegesis simply means trying to get to the correct interpretation and meaning of the portions in question. It also means to get to the correct understanding of the portion. Here we are going to do a word for word study of this verse; so let's get into it straight away, even though we do not have time to do a thorough study of this verse.

**"You have been weighed on the scales and found wanting."**

## 3.1 YOU

This is a direct confrontation to the king. It could also mean you and I personally – today – all who are reading this book. God is talking to us today, are we listening? The Gospel is a personal thing – a personal, intimate relationship with Jesus Christ. You alone are responsible for your own soul. Don't let this opportunity pass you by. Come to Christ now, and let Him be your Saviour.

## 3.2  HAVE BEEN

This is the past tense. It has happened already. God has looked at your life and compared it with the information you have in your Bible and looked to see if you have followed it, even if you have made mistakes carrying it out. God want to see if you are genuinely trying to follow His Son. The Cross is in the past – have you availed yourself of what Jesus came to do for you? Tomorrow is the future, but tomorrow may not be for you and I. Today is the hour of your salvation – take it before it is too late.

## 3.3 WEIGHED

This is an act of comparison between a set of standards and that which balances it on the other side. You cannot come to Jesus by works. Jesus is the only door to everlasting life with God. When will we be weighted? At the end of the age, at the time of the great white throne mentioned in Revelation. I plead with you to ensure that you are right with God and Jesus as soon as possible, if you are not so already. Just by going to church does not guarantee you a place in heaven – only a commitment to give your life to Jesus will do that.

## 3.4 ON THE SCALES

To be able to weigh, one has to have a set of scales to weigh with, and that set of scales for the Christian is the Holy Bible, from Genesis right through to Revelation. It is all God's Word and it is true and faithful and trustworthy. Right throughout the Scriptures are rules and regulations, and conditions for correct living – between man and man as well as between man and God.

For the Christian it is well to study the full Sermon on the Mount given by Jesus to His disciples. A good book to read on this subject is **Studies in the Sermon on the Mount** by D. Martyn Lloyd-Jones. The Sermon on the Mount is all about kingdom living and is very important, otherwise Jesus would never have given it to His Disciples.

## 3.5. AND FOUND WANTING

This is something we all do not want to have against us – that we will one day be found wanting and stand bowed head before the Judge, who is Jesus Himself. There are four areas where we may be found wanting:

a. In us as individuals
a. In us as families
b. In our sanctuaries, i.e. our churches, and
c. In us as a country.

In all these areas in general we are found wanting, but it starts with the individual first. Is God pointing a finger at us? Is there perhaps writing on the wall for us to take heed of? Just the other day on my way back home from church, the number of cars at a well-known supermarket gave me no indication that our country is country of worshippers, as we claim it to be. Video shops with racks of vulgar and vile movies are full of people queuing to spend their Sunday at home, filling themselves and their families with smut and filth. And it is getting worse by the year!

Where is it all going to end? At the Great White Throne, so get yourself ready now!

In conclusion: Could Belshazzar have avoided the collapse of his empire? If he had only humbled himself there and then before God, as his father Nebuchadnezzar had done before. We always think that our fathers knew nothing; how wrong can we be! Many proud people are walking around who know that they are going to hell, and really don't want to go, but are too proud to admit it and "lower" themselves in confession and commitment to Jesus.

This interpretation by Daniel is beautifully summed up in 2 Chronicles 7:14-15: *"If my people, who are called by my name, will humble themselves and pray and seek my face and turn from their wicked way, then will I hear from heaven and will forgive them their sin and will heal their land. Now my eyes will be open and my ears attentive to the prayers offered in this place."*

God would never have given Daniel the interpretation of the writing on the wall had his own life not been pure and clean. It is quite clear that Daniel, through all the problems of living in a godless society, had still not defiled himself with heathen practices. How did he do it? Only by letting himself be strengthened by God and the Holy Spirit.

Let us revive ourselves today, and then let us go out and bring the Gospel of the kingdom of God to our families, our church and then to our beloved country, so that God may bless all of us.

# CHAPTER 9

**Daniel 6:1-3**

*1.    It pleased Darius to set over the kingdom an hundred and twenty princes, which should be over the whole kingdom;*

*2.    And over these presidents; of whom Daniel was first: that the princes might give account unto them, and the king should have no damage.*

*3.    Then this Daniel was preferred above the presidents and princes, because an excellent spirit was in him, and the king thought to set him over the whole realm.*

We ended the previous chapter on the lifestyle of Daniel just after he had given the message of the writing on the wall. We saw how it applied to us as well, in our time today. We have to be ever careful and cautious about our way of life. We must be sure that verse 27 of chapter 5 applies to us as little as possible, and that the quality of our living is also high as humanly possible.

If we do not take note of this, that verse will come back to us and say; *"You have been weighted in the scales and found wanting."* Walk the way God wants you to walk and that finger will not point at you.

How do we know what God wants of us? There are many Scriptures that point the way, but to single out one portion I would recommend you read Ephesians Chapters 4, 5 and 6 for a start. Write these references down and study them with a new vision and diligence. They will enrich your life tremendously.

I would like to single out a particular set of verses in Ephesians chapter 5 and they are verses 8-10, which says: (and Paul is talking to believing Christians) *"For you were once darkness, but now you are light in the Lord. Live as children of the light (for the fruit of light consists of all goodness, righteousness and truth) and find out what pleases the Lord.*

Verse 10 of Ephesians chapter 5 is of utmost importance. We have to find out what pleases the Lord, and his means delving into God's Word with a searching heart, asking the Holy Spirit to guide and enlighten you, and if you have a searching heart it is imperative that you search the Scriptures with the help of the Holy Spirit. Let God speak to you through His Word.

# 1. Daniel's Trustworthy Style of Work

Looking at Chapter 6 of the book of Daniel we find ourselves now in another era of Daniel's life. Each era bringing its own type of problems and blessings. Just look back on our own life span and we find that we also have lived in different eras, each with its own problems and blessings. King Belshazzar is dead and now king Darius is sitting on the throne. We notice that Daniel is kept in his newly appointed position of the third highest ruler in Babylon.

One thing about Daniel is that whatever situation he is in, and whatever job he is given to do, he does it with distinction and with honour. To whose honour does he do it? Definitely not for himself! He gives all the honour to his God Jehovah.

When we honour God in all our dealings, God honours us as his children of the kingdom. If you are or have been, a father you will know what I am talking about. If your child has been naughty he gets a spanking, but if he has been good, and stays good, then there is peace in the home and there is no need to dish out any more punishment! That alone is a blessing.

Daniel worked in all honesty and obedience to the king in all his work as administrator such that the king planned to promote him to the second highest position in the empire of Babylon. Truly Daniel was a man of integrity let us also try to copy Daniel as far as our own integrity is concerned.

## 2. Professional Jealousy

**Daniel 6:4-5**

> 4.     Then the presidents and princes sought to find occasion against Daniel concerning the kingdom; but they could find none occasion nor fault; forasmuch as he was faithful, neither was there any error or fault found in him.
> 5.     Then said these men, we shall not find any occasion against Daniel, except we find it against him concerning the law of his God.

Once again we come into the realms of professional jealousy. I am sure many of you have at some time or other had the same experience at work or in the church work, etc. it certainly is not a pleasant situation to be in. Daniel once again was of such a character that the satraps and the other administrators could not find fault with his work.

This tells me that Daniel did not steal anything from work to use at home. It tells me that he did no underhand dealings and conniving and bribing, or taking of bribes.

He was, as the scripture records of him: *"They could find no corruption in him, because he was trustworthy and neither corrupt nor negligent."* What a wonderful witness to have as a person! Let us try to be like that.

Once again the people's only resort to finding fault with him was with his relationship with God. I cannot stress it enough that if you and I have Jesus as our Saviour then we have to live that type of life we profess to live. We must not be ashamed of it, nor ought we to be apologetic for it. As the Scripture says: *"Be bold, be strong, for the Lord thy God is with thee."* If Daniel could do it, so can we, with even more boldness, because we have the permanent indwelling of the Holy Spirit in us.

Don't let the world point a finger at our lifestyle. Live the godly lifestyle at home, as well as in the open. Someone once said that only when he saw that a particular person was living a completely godly lifestyle at home would he recognize that Jesus truly was in his heart.

You see, so often we pretend to live a godly life in the eye of the public, while at home we are far from God. If you live a sanctified life in secret it cannot be otherwise that you will live a sanctified life in the open. A tree has to be known by its fruit.

# 3. The Accusation – Deceitfully Done!

**Daniel 6:6-9**

> 6.   Then these presidents and princes assembled together to the king, and said thus to him, king Darius, live for ever.
> 7.   All the presidents of the kingdom, the governors, and the princes, the counsellors, and the captains have consulted together to establish a royal statute, and to make a firm decree, that whosoever shall ask a petition of any God or man for thirty days, save of thee, O king, he shall be cast into the den of lions.
> 8.   Now, O king, establish the decree, and sign the writing that is be not changed, according to the law of the Medes and Persians, which altereth not.
> 9.   Wherefore king Darius signed the writing and the decree.

One thing you will notice in these verses is that when the accusation against Daniel was made it was not made directly about or to him. It was done in a very round about way. It was done in a way that favoured the king himself, and that made the king feel he was exalted above everything else. Satan's way, even today, is to make his victim feel that he is above the living God, that he can do it on his own without God's help.

Notice also just how this great group of high officials had gathered together without the knowledge of

Daniel himself. It was all so hush-hush that apparently Daniel did not have a hint of what was happening behind his back. What happened then still happens today. Have you ever taken part in such a conspiracy?

It was in this state of flattery that they very cleverly enticed the king into signing the decree that would have a profound effect on Daniel and his fellow Hebrew exiles. Be ever watchful for the traps that Satan sets for the Christian and any other who would seek the loving kindness of Jesus in their life.

## 4. Daniel Ignores the King's Command

**Daniel 6:10-12**

> 10. *Now when Daniel knew that the writing was signed, he went into his house; and his windows being open in his chamber towards Jerusalem, he kneeled upon his knees three times a day, and prayed and gave thanks before his God, as he did aforetime.*
> 11. *Then these men assembled, and found Daniel praying and making supplication before his God.*
> 12. *Then they came near, and spake before the king concerning the king's decree; Hast thou not signed a decree, that every man shall ask petition of any God or man within thirty days, save of thee, O king, shall be cast into the den of lions? The king answered and said, the thing is true, according to the law of the*

*Medes and Persians, which altereth not.*

*"Now when Daniel learned that the decree had been published, he went home to his upstairs room where the windows opened towards Jerusalem. Three times a day he got down on his knees and prayed, giving thanks to his God, just as he had done before."*

Daniel, the man of God that he was, never let his God down, he was a man with a mission and of steadfast nature – nothing seemed to shake him off course. Up to a few years ago [1988] I used to do a lot of sailing and my dingy could go nowhere nor do anything without the dagger-board to give anchor in the water, nor the rudder to do the steering. One needs a goal to steer to otherwise it all turns out to be a senseless way of spending the day.

Daniel had a goal in his life – God. Without God in his life the Book of Daniel would never had been written. Daniel never neglected his prayer life, even in time of great danger. Many people only turn to the Lord when thy happen to be in hot water. Of course, praying in an emergency is better than not praying at all. When Peter walked on the water and began to sink, he did right in crying out to Jesus to save him. (Matth 14:30)

Jonah is to be commended for praying inside the belly of the big fish, (Hebr – gad ha-gadol = big fish. A whale is never mentioned in the original Scripture} even though he was in that "tight spot" because of his own disobedience (Jonah 2:1) The Lord answered both Peter and Jonah. But when things are going against us or going for us, it should not make any difference. Prayer should be the natural part of our lives that we engage in, no matter what the circumstances – good or bad.

Our Scripture lesson illustrates this truth. The enemies of Daniel had gone to Darius the king of Babylon, and encouraged him to sign a document which, according to the Law of the Medes and the Persians, could not be changed. The decree stated that for 30 days anyone who asked a petition of any god or man other than from the king himself would be thrown into a den of lions.

Even though Daniel knew this, he kneeled three times a day, and prayed and gave thanks before his God, as he had done previously. These last five words tell it all. Daniel's emergency prayer reflected his consistent devotion to the Lord. Although the Father welcomes our petitions in a crisis. He takes even greater delight in our thankful prayers when all is going well. Whatever the circumstances, therefore, whether this is good day or a bad day, make prayer a vital part of your life. Have you talked with God to day?

In conclusion, I would like to leave this thought for the day:

**"If you want to know how to pray in hard times,
practice praying in good times."**

# Chapter 10

We come now to one of the most famous or well-known passages in the whole of the Bible. Very few have never heard of it in some form or other. Many have given sermons on the event itself, but few have majored on the events around the incident itself. We will be examining the event itself as well as the events surrounding it, i.e. the before and after.

Daniel's unceasing prayer life should be a constant encouragement to us in this time. Prayer should be the constant companion of the believer and as we study the lifestyle of Daniel, we see that prayer was the great power in his life. Men of prayer are always in a position of spiritual power. In this setting we study what happened to Daniel under pressure.

# 1. Daniel under Pressure

**Daniel 6:13-14**

> *13.     Then answered they and said before the king. That Daniel, which is of the children of the captivity of Judah, regardeth not thee, O king, nor the decree that thou hast signed, but maketh his petition three times a day.*
>
> *14.     Then the king, when he heard these words, was sore displeased with himself, and set his heart on Daniel to deliver him: and he laboured till the going down of the sun to deliver him.*

Here we see that the men went in as a group to bring the accusation to the king that Daniel was not obeying the decree that had been issued. It is said that there is strength in numbers. If one person complains about something then very little notice is taken about it because the assumption can be made that if all the others do not complain then the majority is happy about the situation. We know for a fact that that is not necessarily so.

Let's take an example from our period here in South Africa. There are thousands of Christians in South Africa of all races. I do not know the exact figures. The majority of the Christians do not approve of certain programs being shown on TV right now, especially when they are shown at prime time when so many children are watching.

If every Christian had to write just one letter to the SABC-TV in complaint, then the SABC-TV will have to do something about it. Why? For the simple reason that they take each letter as representing a certain number of the population, let's say 1000. They assume for example that only one out of every 1000 people actually write in to complain. Therefore if only 1000 people write in, stating the reason for their complaint, they are taken to represent one million people, and that's a lot of complaining to content with.

What do you and I do about it? Do we write in? I must confess that I personally am one of those who do not. I often want to, but somehow it keeps being put off. Why don't we unite and do something about it.

Notice the clever way the group came to the king and got king Darius to first confirm the decree before actually bringing Daniel's name in as the culprit. In verse 14 we read that the king was greatly distressed when he heard that it was Daniel. It is obvious here that king Darius had great regard for Daniel and considered him worthy to make an effort to release him.

Although the Scripture does not go into detail of just how the king tried to save Daniel from the sentence, it is almost certain that he had a face to face talk with Daniel to persuade him to go with the decree and so save his life. It must have been a long and hard discussion because the group again

125

approached the king and reminded him that under no circumstances may the law be broken, not even by the king himself.

When I read that the king was determined to save Daniel, and that he had made every effort until the going down of the sun, it tells me what a tremendously strong character Daniel had. He stood fast and steady as a rock for God in the face of the death sentence. This is how we should take our stand, full of the Spirit and in the strength of Jesus. After this king Darius had no option open to him but to give the order to throw Daniel into the lion's den.

## 2. Daniel Sentenced to Death

**Daniel 6:15-17**

15. *Then these men assembled unto the king, and said unto the king, Know, O king, that the law of the Medes and Persians is. That no decree nor statute which the king established be changed.*

16. *Then the king commanded, and they brought Daniel, and cast him into the den of lions. Now the king spake and said unto Daniel. Thy God whom thou servest continually, he will deliver thee.*

17. *And a stone was brought, and laid upon the mouth of the den; and the king sealed with his own signet, and with the signet of his*

*lords; that the purpose might not be changed concerning Daniel.*


In these verses we see the result of this united effort to discredit Daniel. Of interest, we read in the New Testament that we have to be obedient to the Government of the land we are in. Now why would Daniel not obey the king's decree?

Ephes. 6:5-8 says this: *"Slaves obey your earthly masters with respect and fear and with sincerity of heart. Obey them not only to win favour when their eye is upon you, but like slaves of Christ, doing the will of God from your heart. Serve wholeheartedly, as if you were serving the Lord, not men, because you know that the Lord will reward everyone for whatever good he does, whether he is slave or free."*

In Timothy 6:1 Paul gives good advice. He says: *"All who are under the yoke of slavery should consider their masters worthy of full respect, so that God's name and our teaching may not be slandered."*

Listen carefully to what Peter told the suffering Christians, remembering also that Daniel was now standing before a den of lions who were just ready to tear him into pieces. In 1 Peter 2:13-17 he pointed out: *"Submit yourselves for the Lord's sake to every authority instituted among men: whether to the king, as the supreme authority, or to governors, who are sent by him to punish those who do wrong and to commend those who do right, for it is God's will that by doing so you should silence the ignorant* talk of foolish men. Live as free men, but do not use your freedom as a cover-up for evil: live as servants of God. Show proper respect to everyone. Love the brotherhood of believers, fear God, honour the king."

In verses 19-20 Peter comes to the main part, and take careful note of what he said. He said: "For it is commendable if a man bears up under the pain of unjust suffering because he is conscious of God. But how is it to your credit if you receive a beating for doing wrong and endure it. But if you suffer for doing good and you endure it, this is commendable before God."

This is exactly what Daniel was doing! He endured the suffering even though he was innocent in God's eyes. Daniel knew that he had to follow God's commands rather than that of the king. We are to keep the laws of the land, but we are not to ignore the commands of God.

By bowing down to idols you not only shame the name of God, but you are also in fact renouncing the rule of God in your life. Daniel loved his God more than anything else, even to the point of death. This brings us to the next point.

# 3. The Execution of the Sentence

**Daniel 6:18-20**

> 18.   Then the king went to his palace, and passed the night fasting neither were instruments of musick brought before him: and his sleep went from him.
>
> 19.   Then the king arose very early in the morning, and went in haste unto the den of lions.
>
> 20,   And when he came to the den, he cried out with a lamentable voice unto Daniel, O Daniel, servant of the living God, is thy God, whom thou serve continually, able to deliver thee from the lions?

As Daniel was thrown to the lions, the king's parting words were: *"May your God, whom you serve continually, rescue you!"* Notice that he said "YOUR God" and not "The God you serve." There is a subtle difference here. It was not just the God of Daniel but YOUR God, i.e. Daniel's God. The king was acknowledging the God and Daniel were inseparable companions. He also recognized that Daniel served the Lord under all circumstances AND CONTINUALLY, all the time!

How is our worship? Do we praise the Lord all the day through? Or do we leave that for Sundays only? Is God REALLY our God, or is He just there for our convenience, like a servant relegated to the kitchen, to be called into our lounge only when we have the need of Him? God and Jesus and the Holy Spirit should be welcome at our side and in us and we should always be aware of Him throughout the day and night.

The night that Daniel spent in the lion's den was most probably the longest night the king had ever spent, and at first light he ran to the lion's den. Before he had even reached the den he was already calling out to Daniel, hoping that he was still alive. His action tells me quite a story! Many people do not want to believe the Word of God, and openly denounce it, yet deep down there is a desire to have the peace of God in their life.

King Darius was one such person. He also had some of the spill-over from Daniel's way of life. When being in the presence of a saint for any period of time, something has to happen! He even acknowledges that Daniel's God is a living God. One lesson we have to learn from here is that when we trust in God and Jesus we are not spared the problems of this life, rather, we are to go through them. Daniel was not spared the inconvenience of the lion's den. He had to go through the night with the lions. When we trust implicitly in God, He watches over us with the help of His angels.

Daniel 6:24

> 24. And the king commanded, and they brought those men which had accused Daniel; and they cast them into the den of lions; them and their children, and their wives; and the

*lions had the mastery of them, and brake all their bones in pieces, or ever they came to the bottom of the den."*

Another lesson is that if we are part of a conspiracy to damage the life of an innocent person, we will surely know the heavy hand of God upon us. Because of the wonderful influence Daniel had over king Darius, the king penned these inspiring words of testimony: *"For he is the living God and he endures for ever, his kingdom will not be destroyed, his domain will never end. He rescues and he saves; he performs signs and wonders in the heavens and on the earth, He had rescued Daniel from the power of the lions."* (Daniel 6:26b-27)

### Daniel 6:28

*28. So this Daniel prospered in the reign of Darius, and in the reign of Cyrus the Persian.*

That testimony can be just as true in your and my life even today. All we have to do is to follow Daniel's example. That is the challenge for you and I. Are we going to take it?

# CHAPTER 11

This Chapter follows closely on Chapter 6, and happened shortly after Daniel's experience in the lion's den. By this time Daniel was able to worship in freedom and by his strong stand and the miracle of coming out of the lion's den would have made him a very famous and respected man.

Because he became respected, the name of God became known among the ordinary people. It would be very interesting to find out, if it were possible, the number of people who accepted the worship of the true God at that time. Maybe we will know one day!

## 1. Daniel's Bible Study

**Daniel 9:1-2**

1. *In the first year of Darius the son of Ahasuerus, of the seed of the Medes, which was made king over the realm of the*

*Chaldeans:*

2. *In the first year of his reign I Daniel understood by books the number of years, whereof the word of the Lord came to Jeremiah the prophet, that he would accomplish seventy years in the desolations of Jerusalem.*

Bible study should be a very important part of the Christians life and is in fact to be part of our life. In the Book of Acts there is a very interesting piece of Scripture that should be memorised by us all, as it is of vital importance to the professing Christian. The Scripture is in Acts 17:11, which reads as follows: *"Now the Bereans were of more noble character than the Thessalonians, for they received the message with great eagerness and examined the Scriptures every day to see if what Paul had said, was true."*

What Paul is saying here that the Thessalonians were of noble character, beautiful Christians, serving the Lord, yet, they and the other churches lack something important to Christian growth, and that "something" is proper enthusiastic Bible Study. The Bereans had this extra zeal, and whatever Paul told them they listened to, and went home and studied to see if what they were told was indeed true.

How is our Bible Study? Do you read the bible every day? And if you do, do you just read it without really asking the Holy Spirit to reveal some truth to you?

Study is vitally important in the growth of each of us. Daniel obviously did a lot of study over and above all the heavy duties of the office as administrator of Babylon. Daniel gives us here the example that there is no excuse for daily Bible Study.

I challenge all of you to start a daily period of Bible Study. If you have not done so already! *"I, Daniel understood from the Scriptures, according to the word of the Lord given to Jeremiah the prophet that the desolation of the Jerusalem would last seventy years."* In other words, the period of exile would soon be over.

Let us read in Jeremiah just what Daniel brought to the Lord in petition. Jer. 25:10-12: *"I will banish from them the sounds of joy and gladness, the voices of bride and bridegroom, the sound of millstones and the light of the lamp. This whole country will become a desolate wasteland, and these nations will serve the king of Babylon for seventy years. But when the seventy years are fulfilled, I will punish the king of Babylon and his nation, the land of the Babylonians, for their guilt." Declares the Lord, "and will make it desolate for ever."*

This brings us to Daniel's petition:

## 2. Daniel's Petition to God

*Verse 3: "So I turned to the Lord God and pleaded with him in prayer and petition, fasting and in sackcloth and ashes."*

This verse has 8 important points to teach us today and each point is worthy of a full message. We do not have that time and space now, so let me quickly summarize them.

### 2.1   I, i.e. ME

Daniel did not leave it for someone else to do. He plunged right into the business of getting done what had to be done. Here is a very busy man making time to do the things of the Lord. Many Christians will have lots of time on their hands for themselves and for the Lord if only they organize their time properly, and with the right priorities. There is no excuse for not spending time in prayer and intercession.

### 2.2   TURNED

To turn is to move in another direction to that which you have just been going. Daniel moved out of the work area he had just been in and turned his attention to what he had just discovered. Daniel did not let any grass grow under his feet. What about you and I? how often do we turn and get things done for the Lord? By not turning, we move away from the blessing of that particular job.

## 2.3  TO THE LORD GOD

Daniel did not turn to ask the advice of his friends: he turned immediately to Jehovah. Only one who lives closely to Jesus asks Jesus for advice throughout the day. Only one who is close to Jesus thanks Him immediately whenever he or she receives blessing at work or elsewhere! During the day, at work, or at home if you are a housewife or a pensioner, do you talk to Jesus as if He is your friend at your side all the time?

## 2.4  AND PLEADED WITH HIM

To plead with someone is actually to go down on your knees or prostrate oneself before the person you are asking the favour of. To plead is also a legal term. An advocate pleads the case of his client before the judge. Here is Daniel, as an advocate, pleading on behalf of God's people, before the Almighty Himself. This tells me that Daniel, in this intense moment of pleading with the Almighty God, was either kneeling or flat on his face before

God. I imagine it would be the latter. Here he is like the parable of the persistent widow in Luke Chapter 18. He pleaded with God until he received an answer.

## 2.5 IN PRAYER

Daniel knew the proper way to come to God, and that was in prayer. Just as there are different ways of asking for something, so there are different ways of praying to God. Arrogant prayer does not even reach the ears of God. Only the humble and contrite and sincere prayer reaches His ears. It is well to note this in our own life. Much has been said about prayer and it's for you to take note and to put it in practice.

## 2.6 AND IN PETITION

To petition is to ask for a change in the present circumstances. My dictionary says this of petition: "A request made for something desired, esp. a respectful or humble request, as to a superior or to those with authority." Daniel and his other Hebrew compatriots have been almost seventy years in exile, a whole generation – a lifetime in the foreign land. By now Daniel was an old man of approximately 85 years old, full of experience and wisdom, and because of this he knew just how to approach his God who had delivered him out of so much trouble. I think very few people realize that when Daniel was thrown into the lion's den he was already in his eighties. At that age he was still a strong and wise administrator for a great Empire.

## 2.7   IN FASTING

This is not just the abstaining of food in the hope of losing weight. This is a genuine intention of thinking of nothing else but the problem, at hand. When the hunger pangs come, it is a reminder that there is a job to do. It was a nudging elbow, if you want to call it that, which kept his mind on what he had to do.

## 2.8   AND IN SACKCLOTH AND ASHES

It is a pity this is not used today. If anything will humble a man more, it is bringing one down to earth from the affluence of our day. Even with the inflation as it is, we live like kings compared to the average person of those days. Who would ever have thought of washing machines, dishwashers, microwave ovens etc. The list is so long that it would reduce the ancients in Daniel's time to tears to hear what we have today.

They had to walk. We ride around in cars in luxury. Sackcloth and ashes reduces one to a low level, and only when we are down to a level where God can talk to us can we hear from Him. Think carefully on what I have just said, because it is a vital part of the true humble Christian. Jesus said that before we may lead, we must first learn to serve. Those who would be first will be last.

In conclusion we see here that Daniel, through experience, knew just how to come to God to get answers to his prayers. Study John 15:1-17 and practice with humility and with a contrite heart, a penitent heart, what Jesus told His disciples.

Don't just read it on the surface. Delve carefully into what Jesus was actually saying. Ask the Holy Spirit to enlighten you as you read these passages. Daniel had found the answer through experience, through actually applying what God had said in His Word.

Let's go out today and apply Daniel 9 verse 3 in our lives as if our life depends on it. Do it with sincerity, believing that God will answer your prayer, but in His own good time. When it is answered, give thanks to the Lord God on High. May you be blessed as you do so!

# CHAPTER 12

In this Chapter we will analyse Daniel's prayer of petition and see just how we can enrich our own prayer life.

Any prayer recorded in the Scriptures is worthy of study. Firstly, it gives us clues as to the character of the one praying and, secondly it gives us clues on how to pray in a particular situation. So often I hear the complaint, "I can't pray, I just don't know where to start or how to start, and I can't pray like so and so."

It is of prime importance that you don't, I repeat DON'T try to copy another's style of praying. Rather come to God in prayer in your own way, and just talk to Him in a natural conversational style. To try to pray in another style, contrary to your character, will only confuse you further, and draw your attention away from Jesus; more so when you are trying to concentrate on copying others. By all means take tips from other Christians, but don't copy! God is looking at the intentions of your heart, and NOT whether you are making grammatical mistakes or not.

As promised, let us analyse Daniel's prayer and see how we can adapt it for our own use. The points I will be bringing forward to you will not necessarily be in strict order in the prayer. Many of them will be intertwined, or woven in, with the others. What we are looking for here are the basic ingredients that make this prayer an outstanding prayer of intercession, in this prayer there are 7 main areas that stand out and are worthy of note, the first being:

## 1. Daniel's Doxology to God

**Daniel 9:4**

> 4      And I prayed to the Lord my God, and made my confession and said, O Lord, the great and dreadful God, keeping the covenant and mercy to them that love him, and to them that keep his commandments."

Before you get a fright at the word doxology let me explain it. Doxology is only a theological word for the act of praising God and/or the act of worship. Praise and worship are actually two different things, but if we combine them in a loose way it would represent the act of paying compliments to God, to speak highly of Him and to Him.

Doxology can take the form of the spoken word, or

of singing your praises. Roget's Thesaurus also says that it is to not spare one's blushes. In other words, one who blushes is normally shy, and not praise God easily in public. If you do not spare the blushes then you will praise God before others.

Remember, Daniel seldom prayed in secret; his window was always open and anyone outside passing by would easily see him at prayers. Daniel praises the God who is great and awesome. Awesome – meaning so wonderful that it is impossible, or had to describe in words, the wonderfulness of the god who overwhelms the mind and the heart.

He is such a wonderful God, He keeps all His promises and the covenant He makes right to the last letter. Our prayer should always begin with praise for the Lord. Praise is in fact giving of yourself to the Lord, and this praising is also a ministry that should be encouraged and developed by the believer as it teaches us to be generous in our giving to the Lord.

## 2. Daniel's acknowledgment of Sin

### Daniel 9:5-6

5 *We have sinned and committed iniquity and have done wickedly and have rebelled, even by departing from thy precepts and from thy judgment.*

6 *Neither have we hearkened unto thy servants*

143

*the prophets, which spake in thy name to our kings, our princes, and our fathers, and to all the people of the land.*

In our modern world the word "sin" has been pushed out of the way. I am not going to go into all the ways sin is talked away, but one thing that cannot be denied, is that sin, no matter by what word you may call it, is a reality just as much as Hell is a place where the unsaved, away from Jesus Christ, will go to. If you talk it away, then you are only fooling yourself to your everlasting detriment. Out of Jesus' own mouth came the oft said words: *"Your sins are forgiven you, go and sin no more."*

To deny sin is to deny the words of Jesus Christ, the Son of God. It is only when you start to acknowledge that sin in your life has to be dealt with, is it possible for Jesus to help you. Daniel understood this only too well. Although he himself led an almost faultless life, he took upon himself the sins of his people in this prayer of intercession. He becomes a type of Christ on the Cross.

If you intercede on behalf of someone else then you should be CARRYING that person's burden to God. It must weigh so heavy on you that you groan and cry before the Lord, pleading for mercy. Daniel, in sackcloth and ashes, lay prostrate before the Lord in agony of soul, just as Jesus sweated great drops of sweat that evening in the Garden of Gethsemane, which in Hebrew means the Place of the Oil Press. Daniel carried the burden of his fellow Hebrew's rebellion, wickedness, the turning aside from their

God Jehovah, their hardened hearts, their deaf ears, etc. What a burden to carry, especially if it is not your own! Praise God for the many Daniels we have in our land today. Are you one?

The other point under this heading is that Daniel acknowledges that God acted rightly in dealing with them about their sin. In verse 11 we read: *"All Israel has transgressed your law and turned away, refusing to obey you. Therefore the curses and the sworn judgments written in the Law of Moses, the servant of God, have been poured upon us, because we have sinned against you."*

## 3. Daniel gives credit to God's Character

**Daniel 9:7-11**

> 7  *O, Lord, righteousness belongeth unto thee, but unto us confusion  of faces, as at this day; to the men of Judah, and to the inhabitants of Jerusalem, and unto that are far off, through all the countries whither thou hast driven them, because of their trespass that they have trespassed against thee.*
>
> 8  *O, Lord to us belongeth confusion of face, to our kings, to our princes, and to our fathers, because we have sinned against thee.*
>
> 9  *To the Lord our God belongeth mercies, and forgiveness, though we have rebelled against him;*
>
> 10  *Neither have we obeyed the voice of the Lord*

*our God, to walk in his laws, which he set before us by his servants the prophets.*

*11 Yea, all Israel have transgressed thy law, even by departing, that they might not obey thy voice; therefore the curse is poured upon us, and the oath that is written in the law of Moses the servant of God, because we have sinned against him.*

When we come to God in prayer we must not forget God's character, because we are to copy God's character into our own life. Why? Because we are made in God's image. Through the fall of Adam, man, although still in God's image, lacks God's character.

The only way man is able to obtain God's character into his or her life is to come to God through Jesus.

It is then when the Holy Spirit comes into the believer and imparts the characteristics of God into his life. What are these attributes? The fruit of the Spirit is one. Mercy, righteousness, faithfulness and many others make up the rest. Verse 9: *"The Lord our God is merciful and forgiving, even though we have rebelled against him."* The more you give God the credit for His character, the easier it will be for you to attain it for yourself.

# 4. Daniel brought to God's Remembrance His Covenant.

**Daniel 9:12-14**

> 12 And he hath confirmed his words, which he spake against us, and against our judges that judged us, by bringing upon us a great evil; for under the whole heaven hath not been done as hath been done upon Jerusalem.
>
> 13 As it is written in the law of Moses, all this evil is come upon us, yet made we not our prayer before the Lord our God, that we might turn from our iniquities, and understand thy truth.
>
> 14 Therefore hath the Lord watched upon the evil, and brought it upon us; for the Lord our God is righteous in all his works which he doeth: for we obeyed not his voice.

We are not able to go into the Mosaic Covenant in this book, but only to say that it is basically split into two parts; the blessings and the curses. The blessings when the children of the Lord follow with all their heart, soul, mind and strength. On the other side are the curses that will be brought into effect when God is rejected and/or His laws are not followed

The seventy years of exile was a direct result of the cutting into effect the curse side of the Covenant. The blessings and curse part is still effective today. When you pray to God, remind Him of His promises, and if you have been obedient, He will honour these promises.

## 5. Daniel's Petition and Intercession.

**Daniel 9:15-16**

> 15 And now, O Lord our God, that hast brought thy people forth out of the land of Egypt with a mighty hand, and hast gotten thee renown as at this day; we have sinned, we have done wickedly.

> 16 O Lord, according to all thy righteousness, I beseech thee, let thine anger and thy fury be turned away from thy city Jerusalem, thy holy mountain: because for our sins and for the iniquities of our fathers, Jerusalem and thy people are become a reproach to all that are about us.

Previously we discussed this very subject on verses 1-3 of Daniel Chapter 9. I am not going to elaborate again on it at the moment. I would, however, like to quote a portion of verse 16: *"O Lord, in keeping with all your righteous acts, turns away your anger and your wrath from Jerusalem, your city, your holy hill."*

Proper intercession can turn God's anger away. In our prayers we must also never forget to pray for others. Pray for others more than for yourself, as this turns self away to where compassion should be.

# 6. Daniel reminds God of His Promises

**Daniel 9:17-19**

> 17  Now therefore, O our God, hear the prayer of thy servant, and his supplications, and cause thy face to shine upon thy sanctuary that is desolate, for the Lord's sake.
>
> 18  O my God incline thine ear, and hear; open thine eyes, and behold our desolations, and the city which is called by thy name: for we do not present our supplications before thee for our righteousness, but for thy great mercies.
>
> 19  O Lord, hear; O lord, forgive; O Lord Hearken and do; defer not, for thine own sake, O my God: for thy city and thy people are called by thy name.

In spite of Israel, Daniel reminds God of His promise that He made through Jeremiah seventy years back. How does he remind God about His promise in this verse? He reminds God of the desolate sanctuary in Jerusalem. What he is telling God is that God needs to bring back the glory of the temple worship to His people.

God's temple in the New Covenant is the body of the believer and that is why we have to look after our bodies and our spirit as well as not grieving the Holy Spirit in us. Daniel exhorts God in a direct way: "O Lord, listen! O Lord, forgive! O Lord, hear and act!"

Because of the intimate relationship Daniel had with God during many, many years was he able to talk to God like that. We must be very sure of OUR relationship with Jesus to talk like that!

In conclusion we have point no.7

## 7. God's Answer to Daniel's Prayer

**Daniel 9:20-23**

> 20 And whiles I was speaking, and praying, and confessing my sin and the sin of my people Israel, and presenting my supplication before the Lord my God for the holy mountain of my God;
> 21 Yea, whiles I was speaking in prayer, even the man Gabriel, whom I had seen in the vision at the beginning, being caused to fly swiftly, touched me about the time of the evening oblation.
> 22 And he informed me, and talked with me and said, O Daniel, I am now come forth to give thee skill and understanding.
> 23 At the beginning of thy supplication the commandment came forth, and I am come to shew thee; for thou art greatly beloved: therefore understand the matter, and consider the vision.

"As soon as you began to pray, an answer was given, which I have come to tell you, for you are *highly esteemed.*" We are able to be highly esteemed in heaven right now. All we have to do is to love Jesus with all your heart, have a personal relationship with Him every day, and then follow Him in complete obedience. How wonderful it will be one day when God can say to you and I: *"Well done, good and faithful servant?"*

# CHAPTER 13

## *The Man in Daniel and Revelation*

### Daniel 10:1-9

1.    In the third year of Cyrus the king of Persia a thing was revealed unto Daniel, whose name was called Belteshazzar; and the thing was true, but the time appointed was long; and he understood the thing, and had understanding of the vision.

2.    In those days I Daniel was mourning three full weeks.

3.    I ate no pleasant bread, neither came flesh nor wine in my mouth, neither did I anoint myself at all, till three whole weeks were fulfilled.

4.    And in the four and twentieth day of the first month, as I was by the side of the great river, which is Hiddekel;

5.    Then I lifted up mine eyes, and behold a certain man clothed in linen, whose loins were

*girded with fine gold of Uphaz.*

*6.     His body also was like the beryl, and his face as the appearance of lightning, and his eyes as lamps of fire, and his arms and his feet like in colour to polished brass, and the voice of his words like the voice of a multitude.*

*7.     And I Daniel alone saw the vision: for the men that were with me saw not the vision; but a great quaking fell among them, so that they fled to hide themselves.*

*8.     Therefore I was left alone, and saw this great vision, and there remained no strength in me: for my comeliness was turned in me into corruption, and I retained no strength.*

*9.     Yet heard I the voice of his words: And when I heard the voice of his words, then was I in a deep sleep on my face, and my face toward the ground.*

We come to another interesting part of the Book of Daniel. Up to now I have not touched on any of the visions he was given by God, or any of the prophecies he was told to write down and tell the people. This vision is different, and because of this I am making an exception, for the very reason that this vision had a very important and lasting effect on the life of Daniel. Although we do not know just how long Daniel lived after the end of the writing of this Book, we do know that he was already in his eighties, a wise old man serving the Lord and also serving the kings he served under with distinction. I personally feel that the Lord gave him this vision not

154

long before he died. God saved the best until last!

As a youngster I used to first eat up the best in my plate of food and then struggled to eat the rest that I did not like, and I had to eat the lot whether I wanted to or not. My father, wise as he was, often told me to first eat up the food I did not like and then the taste of the best food will linger long in my mouth after the plate was clean. How right he was, but being stubborn it took me a long time to realize that he was right. The same with our heavenly Father; He tells us things, but, being stubborn, we do not listen either, until it is almost too late, or for some, until it IS too late!

Why is it that we hear but we do not listen? If only we would do immediately what God tells us to do, it would save a lot of heartache. Daniel, on the other hand, obeyed God to the letter, and he took to heart all that God had said to him. Daniel received a revelation which disturbed him immensely, and the result he mourned for three weeks, eating only the cheap common food; no wine or meat. He did not even use any lotions, and we think that Roll-on is modern!

It was in this condition of semi-fasting that God gave him the vision of a life-time. I think it is of importance that we study this vision as it also has importance for us today, just as it had for Daniel and all who have read this Book since that time.

Let us take a look at Daniel's vision:

## *Who was the Man Daniel saw?*

Some have said that it was Gabriel, others say it was Michael. It cannot be the angel Michael because in verse 21 of Chapter 10 the man dressed in linen said that only Michael supported him in a particular incident. It also cannot be the angel Gabriel because on two recorded occasions Daniel had seen Gabriel and there was nothing of special note, except perhaps for the first occasion.

The first was in Chapter 8:16: *"And I heard a man's voice from the Ulai calling, 'Gabriel, tell this man the meaning of this vision.' And he came near the place where I was standing, I was terrified, and fell prostrate."* Nothing was said of how Gabriel looked. Daniel merely fell to the ground because he was in the presence of the chief of God's angels. How would you or I react in that situation?

In the second, in Daniel 9:21, Daniel only recorded: *"while I was still in prayer, Gabriel, the man I had seen in the earlier vision, came to me in swift flight about the time of the evening oblation."*

Of significance in our reading is the fact that Daniel describes the Man that now faces him. This vision is a special vision in that it was given to him in broad daylight in front of those in attendance with him.

That the vision was real is signified in that those around him ran away and went into hiding.

A very special vision indeed!  Who is this man? Maybe you have already guessed! Maybe we must compare this vision given to Daniel to that given to John on the island of Patmos in the Book of Revelation.

## 1. The Man was Dressed in Linen

**Revelation 1:12-13**

> *12.  I turned to see the voice that spake with me. And being turned, I saw seven golden candlesticks,*
>
> *13a. and in the midst of the seven candlesticks on like unto the Son of Man, clothed with a garment down to the foot, ...........*

The robe Jesus was wearing was also of linen, white bleached linen. How do I know that? Jesus being our High Priest was dressed in His priestly clothes. In Exodus 39:37 we read: *"For Aaron and his sons, they made tunics of fine linen."* Aaron and his sons were priests in the service of God. In Chron. 5:12 the Word tells us that the Levites worked at the altar in fine white linen.

Peter tells us that the believer is part of a holy priesthood, and this is confirmed in Rev. 3:4-5 where Jesus said: *"Yet you have a few people in*

*Sardis who have not soiled their clothes. They will walk with me, dressed in white, for they are worthy. He who overcomes will, like them, be dressed in white. I will never blot out his name from the book of life."* John tells us that the overcomer is the one who has overcome the temptations of the world and who has acknowledged Jesus Christ as his Saviour.

Fine white linen is the symbol of righteousness. I pray that all who are reading this book will come to Jesus and be dressed in righteousness.

## 2. The Man had a Belt of Gold around His Waist.

**Revelation 1:13b**

> *13b.      ........and girt about the paps with a golden girdle sash around His chest. "*

There is a subtle difference here and it is this: Both had a belt or sash of gold, which signifies more than royalty, someone of great importance – a King.

The man before Daniel had the golden sash about His waist. This meant that it was being used to tie up part of the clothing, the long flowing section of the lower robe. Although Jesus is our High Priest, His sash did not correspond to the sashes used by Aaron and his sons. Exod. 39:29 tells us that those sashes were of finely twisted white linen and twisted or woven into it were yarns of blue, purple and scarlet. Blue representing heaven where God is, Purple the colour of royalty, and Scarlet the blood of the shed blood of the sin-offering – the blood of the Messiah yet to come. This sash represented service to the God Jehovah they served.

Normally the gold sash indicated the Royal Person who is to be served. The sash is usually placed over the one shoulder and crosses over and covers the chest area. Because this golden sash was about the waist, it says that this Man, although Royal, was in the mode of serving others. This is exactly what Jesus did right up to His ascension into heaven. Now, TODAY, that gold sash is around His chest, diagonally across and over the one shoulder, representing us as High Priest, but more so as King of all.

Indeed He is King of kings and Lord of lords. Is He that to you?

## 3. The Man had a body like Beryl

What does this mean? Beryl is a type of Silicate (Beryllium Aluminum Silicate) which is known for its brilliance, and also its translucency or transparency, and is normally green in colour, but can also vary from blue, blue-green, even to a red and gold colour. I asked the Holy Spirit to guide me as to what it meant.

After a lot of research I was given the following:
In Rev. 21:20 we read that the foundations of the New-Jerusalem are to be decorated with twelve different types of precious stones, and one of them, the eighth, is the Beryl.

The body constitutes the most part of the human frame, and as such, this part houses all the vital organs for life-sustaining functions. Beryl, being transparent, will show these internals, such as faith, love, obedience, in fact, all the fruit of the Spirit. None is hidden in this Body. So we, as the body of Christ, should be showing the same attributes, if we claim to be in Christ.

Beryl is green and this also tells us something. Green signifies several things among others it indicated life and growth. New leaves are a beautiful green. Green indicates vitality and vigour. David, in Psalm 52 said this of himself: *"I am like and olive tree flourishing in the house of God."* Some translations say a green olive tree; others say a sheltered or a luxuriant or strong olive tree. All symbolize just what Jesus is.

The bluish Beryl signifies the heavens – God's dwelling place. (1 Kings 8:30)

Jesus said: *"I am: and ye shall see the Son of man sitting on the right hand of the power, and coming in the clouds of heaven."*

As professing Christians we are to let Jesus' light in

us, shine OUT, through our Beryl bodies, to those in the world. Let them SEE the faith, the love, the obedience IN us. Let us be green trees planted by the waters. Let us go out into the world, searching for the lost. Use this vitality for the furtherance of the kingdom of God.

In the next chapter we will consider the rest of the vision, but in the meantime strive to be dressed in white linen, which is the righteousness of the saints. Let our foundation be faith, love and obedience to our Saviour. Let us remember that Jesus, with the gold sash around His shoulder, is the King of kings, and the Lord of lords.

## 4. His Face was like Lightning

Rev. 1:14 does not specifically mention Jesus' face but says: *"His head and hair were white like wool, as white as snow,"* while Daniel 10:6 tells us that the Man's face was like lightning. Both indicate that the brightness and the whiteness was the climax of the attributes. It is indicating that the face is like the sun shining in all its brilliance. No wonder all who have looked on him fell to the ground!

The Scriptures have some very interesting things to say about this brilliance. Exod. 34:29-35 relates that when Moses came down from Mount Sinai with the stone tablets, after he had spoken with God, and had been in His presence, he also had a special experience. Verses 33-35 says this: *"When Moses* finished speaking to them, he put a veil over his face. But whenever he entered the Lord's presence to speak with him, he removed the veil until he came out. And when he came out and told the Israelites what had been commanded, they saw that his face was radiant. Then Moses would put the veil back over his face until he went in to speak with the Lord."

In the second letter to the Corinthians, Paul had this to say in 2 Cor. 3:13: "We are not like Moses, who would put a veil over his face to keep the Israelites from gazing at it while the radiance was fading away." Paul mentioned further inverse 18; "And we, who with unveiled faces all reflect the Lord's glory, are being transformed into his likeness with ever-increasing glory, which comes from the Lord, who is the Spirit."

May you all partake of the Lord's glory, so that you to may radiate His glory through your face to others.

## 5. The Man had Eyes like Flaming Torches

Rev. 1:14 says that Jesus had eyes of blazing fire. The eyes are one of the most important parts of the body. It is the place where the internal emotion is expressed to the outside world, from the most subtle twinkle in the eye to the extreme obvious, such as hate, sorrow, etc. it has been said that the eye is the window to the soul of that person. Jesus said in Matth. 6:22 "The eye is the lamp of the body. If your *eyes are good, your whole body will be full of light. But if your eyes are bad, your whole body will be full of darkness. If then the light within you is darkness, how great is that darkness."*

It is vital that we use our eyes correctly, so that it will be pleasing to the Lord. To use them to view pornography for instance, will surely send the Holy Spirit away from you in double quick time. Cruden's Concordance tells me that the eye is: "The organ of sight by which visible objects are discerned, and which also shows compassion, fury, vengeance or pardon and gentleness." The concordance has many entries about the eye and mentions many different types of eyes, including the bad eyes and the good eyes. Look them up and you will find interesting research material for many hours.

One of the most exiting verses about the eye is in Proverbs 15:3: *"The eyes of the Lord are everywhere, keeping watch on the wicked and the good."* Daniel talks of seeing eyes as lamps of fire, while Revelation talks of eyes as flames of fire. Both are essentially saying the same thing. A single flame from an oil lamp can only penetrate the darkness to a certain degree, but a large flame that is blazing will penetrate a great distance into the darkness. The inference here is that God can see much further than we can ever see with our small eyes. His eyes pierce the darkness and He knows and sees all the moves we, the believer, as well as the unbeliever, make. Nothing is ever hidden from Him.

One of the most exciting events that involves the eyes will play off in the future, is when Jesus will return to the earth the second time, Rev. 1:7 says: *"Look he is coming with the clouds, and every eye shall see him, even those who pierced him, and all the peoples of the earth will mourn because of him."*

Will you be one that will rejoice? I certainly pray that you will not be the one who will mourn, because at that time it will be too late to change!

## 6. The Man's Arms and Legs gleam like Burnished Bronze

**Revelation 1:15**

> 15.     *And his feet like unto fine brass, as if they burned in a furnace*

And just what does it mean?

In the time of the Old Testament there was the stone-age, the iron-age, and then the bronze-age. In Daniel's time, and even later, bronze was the major metal because it did not rust. I found that bronze signifies three things in the Scripture.

### 6.1  Stubbornness in Sin

In Isaiah 48:4 God said of Israel: *"For I knew how stubborn you were; the sinews of your neck were*

164

*iron, your forehead was bronze."* The people were so stiffnecked and their minds so set that they would not turn from their sin back to the presence of Jehovah. God said that He had made Jeremiah a tester of metals in Jer. 6:26-28; *"I have made you a tester of metals and my people are the one that you may observe and test their ways. They are all hardened rebels, going about to slander. They are bronze and iron; they act corruptly."* Please don't be like bronze and iron in your ways, resisting the call of Jesus on your life. Obey the call of Jesus and open your heart to Him. Get rid of the iron and bronze in your life!

## 6.2 Judgement

God often used war to execute judgment against Israel and other countries. The exile situation that Daniel was in was one such occasion. When king Nebuchadnezzar had his dream of the statue of gold, silver and bronze, and the feet of iron and clay, it is said that the bronze section was the Grecian Empire with Alexander the Great. He was a mighty warrior and most of his weapons were of bronze and brass. In Zech. 6:1: *"I looked up again – and there were before me four chariots coming up from between two mountains – mountains of bronze."*

In the Book of Micah 4:13 we have a definite indication that bronze symbolizes judgment when we read: *"Rise and thresh, O Daughter of Zion, for I will give you horns of iron; I will give you hooves of* bronze and you will break to pieces many nations." If we continue to live in or with sin, then God's bronze will be upon us, and slowly grind us, but if we repent, God's love will abound in our life.

## 6.3 The Infinite Power of Jesus Christ

Jesus will be the Great Judge that will judge the living and the dead at His second coming Rev. 20:11-12: *"Then I saw a great white throne and him who was seated on it. And I saw the dead, great and small. Standing before the throne, and books were opened. The dead were judged according to what they had done as recorded in the books."*

Speaking of Jesus, Peter, in Acts 10:42-43 said this: *"He commanded us to preach to the people and to testify that he is the one whom God anointed as judge of the living and the dead. All the prophets testify about him that everyone who believes in him receives forgiveness of sins through his name."* should we not want to stand before the Judge and be sent to an everlasting prison sentence to the place called Hell, then we must ensure that we continually strive to lead a pure life in Christ. Prov. 3:1-2: *"My son, do not forget my teaching, but keep my commandments in our heart, for they will prolong your life many years and bring you prosperity."*

# 7. The Man had a Voice like the Sound of a Multitude

**Revelation 1:15**

> *15b. ......and his voice as the sound of many waters*

Job 26:14 says: *"How faint the whisper we hear of him! Who then can understand the power of his thunder?"* Ezekiel 10:15 says, *"The sound of the wings of the cherubim could be heard as far away as the outer court, like the voice of God Almighty when he speaks."* In Ezekiel 1:24-25 we read: *"When the creatures moved, I heard the sound of their wings, like the roar of rushing waters, like the voice of the Almighty."*

When God speaks, we should be obedient. We should hear and listen! Jesus is still calling to all who would accept Him. Rev. 3:20 reminds us:

Is He perhaps knocking on the door of your heart today, at this moment?

Won't you open the door and let Him in?

# CHAPTER 14

## *1. He Touched Daniel*

### Daniel 10:10

10.  *And, behold, an hand touched me, which set me on my knees and upon the palms of my hands.*

The touch of God on anyone is one of the most wonderful things that can happen to a person. In Isaiah 6:7 a live coal was touched to Isaiah's mouth and he was told: *"See, this has touched your lips; your guilt is taken away and your sin atoned for."* The touch of God on Isaiah's life started him off on a wonderful course in the Lord, so much so that the Book of Isaiah became the longest in the whole of the Bible.

Jesus did a lot of touching and miracles happened. Matth.8:3 says: *"Jesus reached out his hand and touched the man, 'I am willing,' he said, 'Be clean!' Immediately he [the man] was cured of leprosy."* There are many such instances of the touch of

Jesus upon those who called upon Him.

Won't you let Him touch your heart today? He can set you on your feet as well.

## 2. The Man called Daniel Highly Esteemed

**Daniel 10:11**

> *11. And he said unto me, O Daniel, a man greatly beloved, understand the words that I speak unto thee, and stand upright: for unto thee am I now sent. And when he had spoken this word unto me, I stood trembling.*

Verse 11: *"Daniel, you who are highly esteemed, consider carefully the words I am about to speak to you."* Once before Daniel was called highly esteemed, and that was when he prayed and reminded God of His promise about the seventy years. Dan. 9:22-23: *"Daniel, I have now come to give you insight and understanding. As soon as you BEGAN [Emphasis mine] to pray, an answer was given, which I have come to tell you, for you are highly esteemed."*

Daniel was so highly esteemed that answers were forthcoming even before he had finished his prayers. How was this possible?

Jesus gives the answer to this in several places; one

of which is in John 15. Talking about the true vine Jesus said: *"Remain in me, and I will remain in you. No branch can bear fruit by itself; it must remain in THE VINE* [Emphasis mine]. *Neither can you bear fruit unless you remain in me."* Daniel did just that! He remained in God, no matter what the circumstances were. To remain in Jesus is to follow Him completely.

## 3. Daniel was told not to be Afraid

### Daniel 10:12-14

> *12.    Then he said unto me, Fear not, Daniel; for from the first day that thou didst set thy heart to understand, and to chasten thyself before thy God, thy words were heard, and I am come for thy words.*
>
> *13.    But the prince of the kingdom of Persia withstood me one and twenty days: but, lo, Michael, one of the chief princes, came to help me; and I remained there with the kings of Persia.*
>
> *14.    Now I am come to make thee understand what shall befall thy people in the latter days: for yet the vision is for many days.*

This reminds me of the time God told the same thing to Joshua just before Joshua went into the land of Canaan to possess it. Quite a few times God told him to be strong and courageous. Why? Because God would be with him at all times,

THROUGH the hard times. Daniel was told not to be afraid because he had seen the vision of Jesus. Instead he was to be full of courage because he was in the hands of the Almighty God.

That message is true today. If we are in Christ, then we are not to be afraid. The opposite of afraid is confidence. When you put your confidence in the Lord, you actually take refuge in Him. Psalm 118:8 says exactly that: *"It is better to take refuge in the Lord than to trust in man."*

In Jesus there is no need to be afraid, even of death.

## 4. Daniel Acknowledges his own Helplessness

**Daniel 10:15-17**

> 15.    *And when he had spoken such words unto me, I set my face toward the ground, and I became dumb.*
> 16.    *And, behold, one like the similitude of the sons of men touched my lips: then I opened my mouth and spake, and said unto him that stood before me, O my Lord, by the vision my sorrows are turned upon me, and I have retained no strength.*
> 17.    *For how can the servant of this my lord talk with this my lord? For as me for, straightway there remained no strength in me, neither is there breath left in me.*

It is only when we acknowledge that we can do nothing without God's help that we can grow in the Lord. Pride is the downfall of man so we have to be on our guard against it. Pride is to say that we do not need God's help; we can do it alone. We must allow God's grace to be part of our life. Grace means the unmerited favour and love of God towards us. Grace can never be your portion unless you claim it in all respects and with reverence toward God.

Won't you place your complete confidence and reliance upon Jesus today?

## 5. The man who Touched Daniel a Second Time

### Daniel 10:18-19

*18.	Then there came again and touched me one liked the appearance of a man, and he strengthened me*
*19.	And said, O man greatly beloved, fear not: peace be unto thee, be strong, yea, be strong. And when he had spoken unto me, I was strengthened, and said, Let my lord speak; for thou hast strengthened me.*

Jesus touched him again and strength was given him. Jesus is our Strength and our Fortress and our Rock. Only in Him are we able to conquer the forces of evil that invade our lives, and try to turn us away from God back to the darkness of the world.

Jesus is our Light and our Life. We are to ask Jesus to touch us daily so that we may be continually strengthened through the Holy Spirit. Every day we should be in the presence of Jesus, because that is the only way we are able to be touched by Him. We NEED His healing touch. You need His touch, but if you keep pulling away you will not be touched by Him.

Won't you move close to Jesus so that He may hold you in His arms?

## 6. The Man who Spoke the Word of Truth

**Daniel 10:20-21**

> *20.    Then said he, Knowest thou wherefore I come unto thee? And now will I return to fight with the prince of Persia: and when I am gone forth, lo, the prince of Grecia shall come.*
> *21.    But I will shew thee that which is noted in the scripture of truth: and there is none that holdeth with me in these things, but Michael your prince.*

What is our Book of Truth today? It is the Holy Bible! Do not neglect the study of God's Word. Don't let man teach you  too much from the Book. Rather, ask the Holy Spirit to help you as you read, to point out what He would have for you. This way the bias of man will greatly be reduced. Be very careful of the bias of man, it can lead you to destruction. By that I mean that you can be lead along a wrong road, to everlasting destruction without you realising what is happening.

Don't take everything for granted. Ask the Holy Spirit to reveal to you what the Scripture REALLY says! Especially on doctrinal matters.

# CONCLUSION

We have come to the end of our study in the godly life of Daniel and I trust that you have been enriched by what you have read and learned. I sincerely hope that you are not the type of Christian that sits in the pews, takes great interest in the sermon, and goes out saying, "What a great sermon that was!" and then promptly forgets everything. Each and every section in the book is for a purpose.

It is of no good just reading a book on how to build up a beautiful muscled body, and wish that you had what the photographs depict. A proportioned muscular body is only obtained by dedicated, regular hard exercise and perseverance. To keep it in trim you still have to exercise regularly.

The same applies to our spiritual life. It is only by doing what the Scripture tells us to do, together with the obedience to the leading of the Holy Spirit in our lives that we will be able to enter into everlasting life with God. It is only the overcomers that will inherit everlasting life.

177

To overcome, says my Dictionary, is **"To get the better of a struggle or conflict."**

You can see that, to overcome, means to defeat Satan, and the temptation to do things contrary to God's commands. To overcome is linked to perseverance, which in turn means a steady steadfast course of action which continues right on to the end. We must never lose sight of the fact that to overcome means a continual battle right up until Jesus calls us to that heavenly home.

In our studies on the godly Lifestyle of Daniel you will notice that he displayed all these qualities and attributes. He was human just like you and I, with all the problems, and temptations that we are subjected to. If he could apply all these in his life then so can we, with the same results.

I challenge you, including myself, to start today and give all of these a test, the same way Daniel did when, as youngster, and his three companions were asked to eat food that was against God's commands. After the testing period was over they were found to be better off than the other captives.

Come to Jesus let him take over your life. Give God's way a genuine test over a period of time, and then examine yourself. You have nothing to lose, but everything to gain.

Daniel and many others did just that and they led a wonderful life in the Lord, despite the conditions they found themselves in.

## Lastly, let us read Daniel 12:9-13

*9. And he said, Go thy way, Daniel; for the words are closed and sealed till the time of the end.*

*10. Many shall be purified, and made white, and tried; but the wicked shall do wickedly; and none of the wicked shall understand; but the wise shall understand.*

*11. and from the time that the daily sacrifice shall be taken away, and the abomination that maketh desolate set up, there shall be a thousand two hundred and ninety days.*

*12. blessed is he that waiteth and cometh to the thousand three hundred and five and thirty days.*

*13. But go thy way till the end be; for thou shall rest, and stand in thy lot at the end of days.*

Daniel is told to go his way, i.e. to go on serving the Lord just as he had done before. We are not to let up serving the Lord all the days of our life. We are to be overcomers. At the time appointed we all will be taken out of this world; some to everlasting damnation, and some to everlasting life forever with Jesus.

Daniel is given wonderful assurance that the time will come when he will be resurrected to be with the Lord forever, to receive his inheritance. What is this inheritance? There are many things the believer in

Jesus can inherit, but the ultimate inheritance was put in a form of a question to Jesus by a certain ruler in Luke 10:25: *"And behold, a certain lawyer stood up, and asked him saying , Master, what shall I do to INHERIT* [Emphasis mine] *eternal life?"*

Daniel was promised this inheritance because he was content with God and with his circumstances. Daniel did not try to escape from Babylon. He believed that God would be with him and help him no matter where he was and whatever circumstance he was in. Many people look at the problem and see nothing else. Daniel saw the problem, but he looked PAST the problem, and saw GOD.

Whatever he did, he found peace in God; the peace that passes all understanding! As Daniel did, so many thousands of years ago you, too, can claim the peace of Jesus in your life. All you to do is to receive Him as your Saviour.

I sincerely pray that you will not neglect this important step in your life. God bless you as you do so!

I trust that you have become spiritually enriched by this study in the Godly Lifestyle of Daniel

# APPENDIX

## A. The Judgement Seat of Christ (2 Cor. 5:10)

*"For we must all appear before the judgement seat of Christ that everyone* [Paul is speaking to the believers] *may receive the things done in the body, according to that he hath done, whether it be good or bad."*

There are two different thrones. No believers will appear before the Great White Throne, and no unbeliever will appear before the Judgment Seat of Christ.

The Judgment of the believer's works, not sin, is under discussion here. His sins have been atoned for and are remembered no more forever. (See Hebrews 10:17) and every work must come into judgment. The result is reward or loss of reward, *"For he himself* [the believer] *shall be saved."* (1 Cor. 3:24-25).

This judgment occurs at the return of Christ for His Church. God refers to every thought, word and deed. Hindrances that will rob you of your greater reward.

## B. The Great White Throne (Rev. 20:11-15)

The footnotes of the "New Scofield Bible describes it as follows: The Final judgment. The subjects are the "dead". As the redeemed were raised from among the dead 1000 years before (5) and have been in glory with Jesus during that period. The "dead" referred to can only be the wicked dead from the beginning of human history to the setting of the great white throne in space. The dead are judged according to their works. The book of life is there to answer such as plead their works for justification. See (Matth. 7:22-23)

Romans 8:1 declares, *"There is therefore now no condemnation to those who are in Christ Jesus, who do not walk according to the flesh, but according to the Spirit."*

### The Hand on the Wall (Daniel 5:24)

#### Man's hand or God's hand?

There is theological controversy here with regard to the hand that wrote on the wall. Some translations say that; a) it was a human hand [New International

Version], and b) it was a man's hand [King James Version], Revised Standard Version, Living Bible]. The Modern Language Bible states that it was God's hand.

Again I examined the original Masoretic Text, as before nowhere does it indicate that it was God's hand. The Hebrew is quite clear that God **SENT** a hand – not His own. We must not forget that God is a Spirit and has no human form. Only Jesus came to us in human form. If it was a theophany the Scripture would have stated that it was the hand of the Angel of the Lord, but it did not!

A theophany is a term that describes an appearance of God to man in a form that man would recognize. There are scriptures in the Old Testament which clearly state that the Angel of the Lord was one of the Triune God – but it is taken to be Jesus himself prior to his later coming to this earth in human form. Every now and then He revealed Himself to some on special occasions.]

Here is an almost direct translation from the Hebrew of Daniel 5:24 – From Adonai was previously (before) sent (a) piece of hand to write (down)judgment (Chastisement, punishment) (to) record (write down.)

Let's put it in a more readable form:

**The Lord previously sent a portion of a hand to write and record the judgment.**

From this it can clearly be seen (and a pity) that the Modern Language translators have deviated so drastically from the original Hebrew text and made their own (wrong) assumptions.

In view of the above I cannot agree with those who emphatically state that is was God's hand that wrote on the wall. He **caused** a hand to write on the wall. Remember, He even **caused** a donkey to speak!

Made in the USA
Middletown, DE
01 August 2021

45153305R00106